CHINA

INDIA

PACIFIC OCEAN

RWANDA

ZAIRE

BANGLADESH

BURMA

THAILAND

SRI LANKA

VIETNAM

KAMPUCHEA

MALAYSIA

PHILIPPINES

BRUNEI

INDONESIA

PAPUA NEW GUINEA

SOLOMON ISLANDS

FIJI IS.

MADAGASCAR

INDIAN OCEAN

AUSTRALIA

TASMANIA

NEW ZEALAND

~AREAS OF RAINFOREST

RAINFOREST

IN ASSOCIATION WITH WORLDFOREST 90

JOHN NICHOL

DAVID & CHARLES
NEWTON ABBOT · LONDON

Text © John Nichol 1990

Designed by
Hammond Hammond

Illustrations by
Oonagh O'Toole

Typeset by Chapterhouse,
The Cloisters, Formby,
England

**British Library Cataloguing
in Publication Data**
Nichol, John *1939*–
　The mighty rainforest.
　1. Tropical rain forest
　　ecosystems
　I. Title
　574.5′2642′0913

First impression 1990
Reprinted 1990
First published in
paperback 1994

ISBN 0–7153–9461–4 H/B
ISBN 0–7153–0218–3 P/B

Printed in The Netherlands,
by Royal Smeets Offset,
Weert, for David & Charles

**The prickly trunk of this tree in the
forest of Trinidad helps to protect
it from the growth of lianas, and
also prevents animals climbing it to
get at the leaves (*Adrian Warren*)**

(PREVIOUS PAGE)
**A brilliant sunset over the forests
of Irian Jaya, the Indonesian part of
an island whose other half is the
country of Papua New Guinea
(*Adrian Warren*)**

(PAGE 1)
**A rare mountain gorilla in Rwanda
(*Adrian Warren*)**

(ENDPAPERS)
**The world showing the major areas
of equatorial rainforest that still
remain.**

■

PAPER AND
THE MIGHTY RAINFOREST

The fate of the environment, and of the rainforest in particular, is now the subject of universal concern, and quite rightly so. Unfortunately, however, in the complex and emotive debate on the environment, facts can become distorted and misconceptions can all too easily arise. Many people reading this book may suspect that the paper industry is contributing to the devastation of the rainforest.

Nothing could be further from the truth. None of the wood used for the manufacture of paper comes from the rainforest, and the reason for this is simple – of the vast number of tree species in the rainforest, very few have the characteristics required for paper manufacture, and the cost of extracting these few would make production unviable. In fact, paper manufacturers in the rainforest region are responsible for recultivating barren areas with new, sustainable forest.

The paper industry overall is remarkably 'Green', involving the production of a natural, biodegradable and totally renewable resource, and the silviculture employed to cultivate the raw material has produced healthy, prospering forests which are putting back ever increasing amounts of oxygen into our atmosphere.

The paper industry has developed a symbiotic, rather than parasitic, relationship with the forest. Paper producers are forest people. Their livelihood and their recreation both depend on a living, growing forest. Quite simply, the forest is their lifeblood, and destroying it would mean environmental and economic suicide.

The future of the paper industry depends on successful management of its forests, just as the future of humanity depends on the successful protection of the rainforest.

This book is printed on a paper called Silverblade Matt, produced by MoDo in Sweden from fully sustainable forests.

**The publishers gratefully
acknowledge the support of
MoDo in the production of
this book.**

CONTENTS

INTRODUCTION
7

1
RAINFORESTS OF
THE WORLD
21

5
THE PEOPLE OF
THE RAINFOREST
88

9
WHAT ARE THE
ALTERNATIVES?
159

2
WHAT IS A
RAINFOREST?
45

6
WHY ARE
RAINFORESTS
IN DANGER?
107

10
WHAT IS BEING
DONE TO HELP?
174

3
ANIMALS OF THE
RAINFOREST
56

7
WHAT
HAPPENS WHEN
RAINFORESTS
DISAPPEAR?
131

ORGANISATIONS
WORKING IN
RAINFOREST
CONSERVATION
198

4
PLANTS OF THE
RAINFOREST
73

8
WHO
CAUSES THE
DESTRUCTION?
144

BIBLIOGRAPHY
199

INDEX
200

INTRODUCTION

TWENTY YEARS AGO ALMOST no one outside specialist academic disciplines used the word 'ecology'. Ten years ago hardly anyone talked of rainforests. Today it seems as though everybody in the world is talking about these subjects. On the face of it, that seems a good thing since it means that far more people are aware of all sorts of environmental interests than was the case a generation ago. But when one examines the complete picture in a bit more detail, two points emerge. The first is that much of what is said in newspapers and on television is more or less incomprehensible unless one happens to have a degree in biology (and another one in advanced computer science), and the other is that constant exposure to a continuous flow of information about a topic results in the brain switching off in favour of something of more immediate interest.

This book is an attempt to show what all the present fuss about rainforests is about in a way that will make you want to keep reading, rather than watching television soap operas.

One of the problems is that rainforests tend to look like a lot of trees standing about doing nothing. In fact they are astonishingly interesting places. I cannot imagine anyone (except perhaps a politician) who could enter a rainforest and remain cold about them thereafter. And the more one finds out about these places, the more interesting they become. You might think that all the jungles are on the other side of the world and have nothing to do with us, but we are intimately bound up with what is happening in them.

All children seem to like jungles. There cannot be many small children who have not played games pretending that the legs of the dining-room table are trees concealing a host of deliciously frightening tigers which might be even more dangerous than their own headhunting brothers and sisters. The pleasure in these games is that you can confuse cannibals with red indians and populate the jungle with everything from lions to great big snakes lying in wait to crush you to death, and even the family pets can be given bit parts. But children become teenagers, and, emerging from this entirely different type of jungle a few years later, they seem to have forgotten about how

Insects are eaten by birds, other insects and even man. Just about every type of animal eats insects, and to survive many of them have developed highly effective camouflage, like this expert from Malaysia (*Peter Tryuk/ The Tropical Butterfly Garden*)

(OPPOSITE)
There are many sorts of forest. Cloud forest is similar to rainforest, but at higher altitude, and therefore cooler, with its own wildlife. Treeferns, rather like palm trees, are typical of this environment (*Adrian Warren*)
■

The orb-web spiders of the tropics are huge and often beautifully marked. The strands of the webs are remarkably strong so that even large beetles are unlikely to break free (*Peter Tryuk/The Tropical Butterfly Garden*)

■

much the idea of a rainforest used to excite them. They have changed, but a real forest is even more exciting than any child could ever imagine.

THE POWER OF THE RAINFOREST

You can feel the potential power of a rainforest nearer home. Pay a visit to your nearest botanic garden and enter the tropical house. It is a cliché to say that the heat and the humidity hit you, but they really do. Walk a few paces from the door and you can almost believe that you have stepped around the world into a real jungle, and even lacking the animals it is an impressive place. Another good alternative is to go to a local butterfly garden for they are sure to have a mini-jungle which actually does contain animals. Large, suitably exotic butterflies flap about, their flight so apparently casual, but if you have ever tried to catch one in the wild you will discover that they are far more alert than they appear. With luck you will be able to observe the most brilliant insects, some as large as your hand. Quail and finches flit elusively through the dripping foliage, and you might even come across a tropical tree frog or two.

Years ago tropical rainforests were always depicted as steaming hells. Certainly, they are hot and humid, but no other environment is so full of excitement and interest. Oddly enough one does not have to battle constantly for one's life with a variety of carnivores and venomous snakes; in fact unless a visitor is willing to spend a lot of time patiently waiting and exploring, the chances are that no animals will be seen except for butterflies. There are plenty of signs that the forest is full of life—sounds are all around. Calls of monkeys and birds can be heard throughout the day and the night, and occasional crashings through the branches above indicate the presence of some animal. I suppose that most people would regard such places as threatening, but in reality there is more to fear in the centre of town at the rush hour.

As with all environments, if you know what you are doing a rainforest is no more dangerous than anywhere else. One can find food there, and a rainforest is a veritable pharmacy, as a multitude of the plants can be used to treat a variety of common complaints. A tropical rainforest must also be one of the easiest places in the world to construct somewhere to live; the materials are all around, and there is little so pleasing as being able to build a complete house in a couple of days. The only aspect that can be something of a problem is that any small injuries seem to take for ever to heal, and after some months in a forest one emerges with sores and cuts on the lower leg and myriad tiny abrasions elsewhere that seem to have been around for ever.

Rainforests are incredibly complicated places. Entering one

Butterfly deep in the Amazon rainforest (*Adrian Warren*)

(RIGHT)
There are probably more insects than any other kind of animal in the jungles. At the right season, caterpillars can be found everywhere. When newly hatched, they eat the shells of their eggs before starting to feed on the leaves of their specific foodplant (*Adrian Warren*)

■

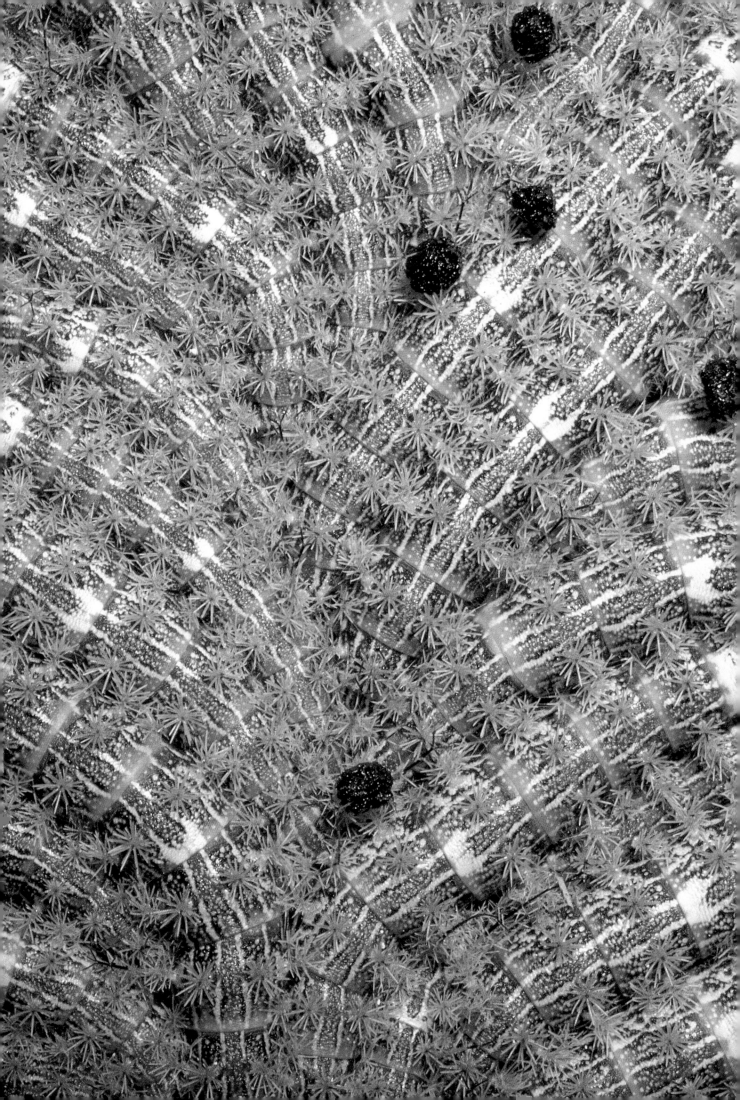

The young leaves of a palm tree in the Amazonian forest of Peru. Young leaves of several jungle trees are red, and in the canopy or from the air such trees often appear to be in flower (*Heather Angel*)

(LEFT)
Tiny settlements are frequently found on the banks of rivers, since these are often the roads of the forests (*Adrian Warren*)

■

for the first time you cannot help but feel the majesty and timelessness of the place. If anything in this world seems permanent it is a jungle, but in fact they are very fragile systems where everything is so interdependent that upsetting one part can lead to unguessed-at damage or even destruction of the whole. And yet there are people who are deliberately destroying the forests.

Many years ago, there was not enough scientific knowledge in the public domain to enable anyone but a specialist to give a reasoned argument for conservation. A speaker had to resort to mumbled comments about aesthetics and morality. Things are different now, and it is possible to show that playing around with one thing can lead to all sorts of frightening and sometimes insoluble problems.

There is so much wrong with the world these days that sometimes one feels that every thinking person must despair. Most international power is in the hands of the politicians and the big multinational companies. The latter in many cases are actively destroying rainforests in the continuing search for megabucks, and how often have you come across any politician worth voting for? Politicians, like lawyers, are incapable of answering straight questions, simply because their thought processes are as contorted as their speeches. On the rare occasion when one of them comes out and declares an interest in the environment, you can bet that what they mean is that they see more votes in that sort of policy, not that they care any more about the world than they did before. Having said that, there are a very few of them that care desperately about our future.

There will always be people like Mother Teresa or Bob Geldof to come along to help the poor of Calcutta or the mass of starving Ethiopians, and thank goodness for it, but to me it seems that the crusade that needs to be taken up above all others, on a massive international scale, is the conservation of the rainforests, for if they go, so does everyone. If our rainforests disappear, you and I will join the lepers of Calcutta and the starving Sudanese.

However, I feel very strongly that it is no use wandering around wailing and preaching doom: that can only be counterproductive. So it was with delight that I agreed to a request in 1988 to organize a very large, very professional international week of high-profile media events in aid of the world's rainforests. Slowly, WORLDFOREST 90 began to take shape.

Right from the beginning it was felt that there should be no preaching. The idea was to organise a variety of different entertainments so that people would want to go to enjoy themselves. By the end of a week of such events everybody in

A ceiba tree, covered in vivid red flowers, attracts numerous insects and hummingbirds, which drink the nectar, collect the pollen and fertilise the tree (*Tony Morrison/South American Pictures*)

(PREVIOUS PAGE)
Flying over the Amazon jungles in a small plane reveals how much there still is (*Adrian Warren*)

■

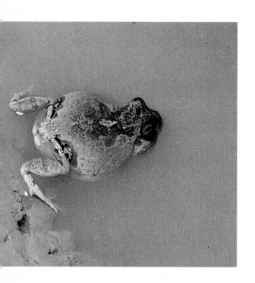

Many frogs are mottled in greens and browns, with brightly coloured undersides. This combination means they are well camouflaged from predators, but when facing a mate the colours can be displayed to advantage (*Adrian Warren*)

∎

the country should be aware of what is happening to the rain-forests of the world, and perhaps think again about how they could help, or indeed what they might do with regard to the many rainforest products they have in their own homes.

Before long the whole idea snowballed and, in addition to all these events, just about every conservation organisation with an interest in the subject was contacted, together with a host of assorted groups throughout the country from primary schools to Women's Institutes, from churches to wildlife supporters' groups. What turned out to be one of the nicest aspects of the whole thing was that WORLDFOREST 90 contained elements that would appeal to everyone. It was about trees and plants, it was about animals of all sorts, it was about timbers and medicines, it was about people and it was about just about anything you wanted it to be. As the organisation began to expand we found that all sorts of people wanted to be involved in some way. At the same time, it was felt that there should be a serious—academic if you like—side to the whole thing, so that too was taken on board. It was decided that the only fair way to dispose of income was to invite applications from any established, bona fide organisation that had an interest in rainforest conservation. Such applications were to be evaluated by the trustees together with experts from various fields. The terms of grants were formulated to take into account all sorts of activities and, so long as they were all designed to have some impact on the conservation of jungles, they were considered relevant.

It was very pleasing in the early days, when it was easy to become despondent, to see the enthusiasm and support that was received from everywhere. When plans for the week of events were revealed most of the conservation agencies were delighted to be involved. They had all been working away for years and had never been able to justify the expense of mounting a consciousness-raising affair—their priority always had to be money. Consequently they were very happy to have an involvement, especially as most of them would be receiving funds at the end of it all.

Generally when a writer comes to acknowledge the many people who inevitably help in the preparation of any book, he mentions those whose involvement has contributed to the book itself. In this case it is different since this book is only part of the whole operation, and so many people who are involved in WORLDFOREST 90 have had an involvement in this book, and vice versa. Consequently it is very difficult to name names since the list would run on for ever. I must however thank by name a few very important people without whom this book would not have happened. First there is Judy, my daughter, and Anne

A bromeliad from the Amazon basin in Brazil has white bases to the leaves in order to guide insects to the flowers. Many plants have lines, coloured areas and spots for the same reason (*Brian Rogers/Biofotos*)

(RIGHT)
Many rainforest trees have enormous buttress roots to support them in the shallow soil (*Heather Angel*)

∎

Three Amazon tribal leaders arrived in London in April 1989 as part of a delegation to talk to the Prince of Wales and other influential people about their plan to extend and protect a Brazilian national park and Indian reserve. The Kayapo Indians' plan will cost 32 million escudos (US$3.6 million) and is designed to provide for demarcation of Brazil's showpiece Xingu National Park Reserve which would be policed by members of the tribe.

The visit by Chief Raoni, Brazil's best known Indian chief, was described by Brigadier Otavio Moreira Lime, the Brazilian Air Force Minister, as 'a revolting spectacle'. The chief was affronted by such language. He also took the opportunity while he was in Europe to visit the Pope and President Mitterrand of France. It was the first time that he had left Brazil, and he was well aware that his European publicity campaign had aroused hostility among the Brazilian establishment.

Ward, who did valuable research for me; Pat Young of
Singapore sent me much material from the Far East that made
my job so much easier; and there are the original members of
the committee of WORLDFOREST 90, Steve and Carole
Hedges, Tim Abrahams and Neil McHugh. Without all their
work throughout, the whole business would not have come off,
neither would this book. To them, thank you, and thank you
also to the very many other people who have helped in so many
ways. Though I cannot name everyone, they are just as
important.

Finally, if the question mark over the future of the
rainforests of this world makes you feel that you would like to
contribute to their conservation, at the end of this book you will
find a list of organisations that are working in this area. All of
them would love to hear from you, either because you wish to
join or work with them, or because you would like to contribute
towards their funds. Alternatively, if you would like to make a
contribution direct to WORLDFOREST 90, the address to write
to is WORLDFOREST 90, 66–68 Rivington Street, London
EC2A 3AY.

Nightjars are superbly camouflaged
birds. They are unusual in that they
are nocturnal, the reason for their very
large eyes (*Adrian Warren*)

(OPPOSITE)
Marine toads are common throughout
Central and South America. They can
grow to a great size and have been
imported into other countries to
control insect pests. In Australia,
where they are known as cane toads,
their populations are increasing
(*Adrian Warren*)

(PREVIOUS PAGE)
Stick insects are extremely difficult to
detect in their natural habitat unless
they move. In some species, males are
very rare indeed and the females lay
fertile eggs without themselves being
fertilised (*Peter Tryuk/The Tropical
Butterfly Garden*)

∎

RAINFORESTS OF THE WORLD

FORESTS OF DIFFERENT KINDS are to be found all over the world. Centuries ago the temperate regions were covered to a great extent in forest, but, as with so many things, a lot of it has disappeared. Much of the temperate deciduous forest was logged to provide useful hardwood, and until recently not many landowners had thought to replace it. The reason for this is not difficult to understand since a hardwood tree can take many decades or even a century before it is considered worth harvesting, although undoubtedly, as pressures for temperate hardwood grows, foresters will suddenly find that the trees can be cut down a lot earlier than they had previously imagined.

The difference between hardwood and softwood does not have too much to do with how hard or how soft the wood actually is, though it is true to say that the descriptions generally hold good. However, to a forester or timber merchant a hardwood tree is what the rest of us call a deciduous tree, while a softwood tree is a conifer.

Because of the length of time it takes for a hardwood tree to reach a marketable size, much of what was previously covered in deciduous forest is now a landscape of conifer forest, though I feel that forest is hardly an appropriate word for the regimented rows of identical trees in a plantation. A real conifer forest such as is found in North America is a totally different animal; there the forests are magnificent living organisms, whereas if you enter a conifer forest in the British Isles you enter a boring, depressing world of straight poles and a carpet of pine needles. I know perfectly well that all sorts of things live in these places; nonetheless they are not nearly as interesting as a natural conifer forest or a deciduous forest. Some years ago I was making a television programme which involved the co-operation of the Forestry Commission in an area a few miles south of

Paradox frogs from South America are so called because (unlike other amphibians) they start life as huge tadpoles, but grow into quite small frogs. Nothing can be taken for granted in the life of the forests (*Adrian Warren*)

(OPPOSITE)
Virunga Forest in Rwanda, home of the mountain gorilla. Many African countries are not too conservation conscious, but Rwanda earns considerable foreign currency from tourists who come to see the gorillas (*Adrian Warren*)

■

Birmingham. The forester who was showing me around took considerable delight in pointing out the plantations, but he clearly felt unhappy at the unkempt, natural forest that lay alongside, and took pleasure in telling me how he would clear it all and turn it into a good commercial plantation as soon as he had the time.

As a result of the demand for native hardwood, chunks of good deciduous forest are now fairly uncommon in Britain, though at last such forests are being extended and replanted, even by the Forestry Commission. But must not Britain have been an attractive place in the Middle Ages, when, so it is said, a squirrel could travel from Bristol to the Wash without coming down to the ground? I have always loved the impression I have of that stupid squirrel rushing backwards and forwards between the two points through the top of the trees.

If you have a chance to visit a temperate deciduous forest, go and explore it for a day. They are fascinating places, full of life of all sorts, and it is so varied. Places like this are often interspersed with clearings, rides or patches of water and the resulting mixture of habitats allows one to find an astonishing variety of plants and animals. There are not many more magical experiences to be had in Britain than to arrive at a place like this just before dawn and watch the forest come alive.

The reticulate python is one of the two largest snakes in the world, though nowadays really big specimens are difficult to find since more and more snakes are being killed for the fashion trade (*Adrian Warren*)
■

Real temperate conifer forests can be just as interesting and full of life, and one cannot pick up a calendar, brochure or tourist guide of North America without finding a picture of one of these forests in the autumn, a rich kaleidoscope of warm colours.

Another extraordinary type of forest is cloud forest, which is to be found at higher altitudes around the tropics. Because of the height above sea level the temperatures are lower than in primary rainforest and consequently the whole character of the place is different. The plants are strange, vaguely different versions of more familiar families, and all of them thrive in high humidity. Many have very delicate foliage, almost feathery in many cases, and ferns abound. A cloud forest in mist is a splendid sight, when each plant between oneself and the horizon can be seen through an increasing volume of mist so that the whole canopy looks like some Chinese painting.

Many terms referring to the natural world tend to be imprecise simply because they refer to living things which are constantly changing, and this is certainly so when we talk about rainforests. We use this term to mean primary rainforest. This we think of as solid jungle but very often one does not find a continuous chunk of rainforest, but one which is interspersed with bamboo forest, patches of water or, increasingly nowadays, patches of agriculture. And perhaps the best term of all is simply 'jungle', though it is one which would make the specialist squirm. Nonetheless for the layperson it conjures up exactly what we mean.

Jungles are only found in a band around the tropics. Northern Australia has a bit left, and the Indonesian archipelago to the north of that country still has considerable forested areas. The Malaysian peninsula is rich in rainforest, and Thailand is still forested in places. Further west one can find it in India, and then there is no more until west Africa. In the Americas much of Central America is forested, and most of tropical South America. It should not be thought however that all these chunks of jungle are homogenous. A South American rainforest is completely different to one in south-east Asia.

Sometimes one sees a very bad feature film with scenes purporting to be in a jungle somewhere which has obviously been stocked from the nearest house-plant nursery. In these jungles one tends to see American *Monstera* plants alongside Asian *Scindapsus*. To be honest, this does not happen nearly as much today as in films that were made a generation ago, though it does sometimes occur in productions that should know better. The best films of all for this sort of mistake are the old Tarzan movies when the trees are alive with Asian reticulate pythons, South American capuchin monkeys and African chimpanzees, all

In 1950, 15 per cent of the earth's land surface was covered by rainforest. Twenty-five years later only half of it was left, and by the year 2000 it is unlikely that there will be more than 7 per cent remaining. If we continue to deplete the rainforests at the present rate we shall be using 4 billion tonnes of wood a year by the year 2000. The amount of forest lost each year is equivalent to a country the size of England.

apparently living together in what is supposed to be an African jungle. To be sure, most people would not notice, but nonetheless each area of rainforest has its own characteristics.

The rainforest of South America, which is to say the Amazon basin, covers two-fifths of this enormous continent. The colossal River Amazon flows through the middle of it, fed by 1,100 tributaries; at the moment there are $2\frac{1}{2}$ million square miles (6.5 million square kilometres) of rainforest in the Amazon basin. One of the problems with rainforests is that they are jam-packed with statistics. When you come to look at them you discover that within their boundaries there are so many records that the mind stalls and can no longer take them in after a while.

THE AMAZONIAN BASIN

The Amazon itself starts as a tiny trickle 17,000 ft (5,000 m) up in the snow-capped Andes mountains whence it flows 4,000 miles (6,400 km) until it enters the Atlantic. It is an enormous river: the mouth is 200 miles (320 km) wide and even 1,000 miles (1,600 km) from where the river meets the sea it is still 7 miles (12 km) in width, and so deep that ocean-going liners can travel 2,300 miles (3,700 km) up its length. The river and the rainforest of which is a part cover nine different South American countries. The whole area is fairly flat, never rising more than 650 ft (200 m) above sea level, and seventeen of the tributaries that flow into the main river are over 1,000 miles (1,600 km) long, which is even longer than the Rhine. There is so much water in the forest that it is useless thinking of travelling by land, and the only sensible way to get about is by boat. The smallest of the boats used, the pirogues, are still made to this day out of hollowed tree trunks, though they usually have additional boards fixed to the sides to provide additional freeboard. These primitive craft are astonishingly unstable and, entering one for the first time, an inadvertent lean to one side can tip you into the river. When a pirogue has been fitted with an outboard motor it is about the most useful way of getting around the area.

Travelling along one of the many wide waterways that penetrate the forest everywhere one finds that boredom easily sets in, since from a distance of a few yards the monotonous wall of jungle with which the river is lined seems endless. But if one is not in a hurry and, instead of rushing along with much noise, one potters quietly along as near to the edge as possible, another world begins to make itself known. If you are lucky, birds can be seen, usually herons of one or another species, but sometimes kingfishers or birds of prey appear briefly. From this vantage point it is just about impossible to see actual land as one has to

As the demand in the Western world for cheap meat increases, more and more rain-forest is destroyed to provide grazing land for the animals that will ultimately end up as hamburgers and other culinary delights. In South America there are 220 million head of cattle, 20 million goats, 60 million pigs and 700 million chickens, while the Far East has 260 million head of cattle.

Production of meat uses 3 billion hectares of land, twice what is used to produce crops of all sorts. Mankind consumes 140 million tonnes of meat a year, or 30 kilograms per person. This average does not represent a true picture, however, since the developed world, which contains over a billion people, consumes 90 million tonnes, while the Third World, with three times as many inhabitants, consumes only half as much.

A waterfall over jasper rocks in Venezuela. The flow of rivers in rainforests fluctuates throughout the year, and can change from a modest trickle to a flood in a short time (*Adrian Warren*)

∎

peer through an impenetrable tangle of mangroves lining the shore. Occasionally there might be a large iguana lying full length along a branch overhanging the water and, although the really big ones tend to stay put unless disturbed, smaller ones tend to panic rather more easily and will sometimes leap straight into the water.

If the tributary you are travelling along is a small one and the sun is not reflecting from the surface, it is usually possible to see right to the bottom as the water is surprisingly clear. When this is the case it is fun to watch the frantic lizard swimming as fast as he can between the subaquatic jungle of fallen branches and tangled roots. Just occasionally one sees a swimming tapir, or perhaps an anaconda, but this is rare since most animals have learnt that it is not a good idea to go anywhere near humans. If you turn your canoe down a small stream or creek you eventually penetrate through the mangrove jungle that lines the bank of the larger waterways and a different world emerges, though the transition is not immediate.

The easiest place to land is often an abandoned site of a former village since the bank at that point is likely to be rather more free of vegetation, and more easily accessible. Wandering about among the abandoned village one can come across a host of fascinating plants and animals. The temperature throughout the area is usually somewhere in the eighties and, as you might imagine, the humidity is very high and as a result everybody is

constantly covered in a film of sweat. This in turn means that often there is a good population of mosquitoes sitting on one's back and shoulders enjoying a feed. At one time this used to bother me enormously since I disliked intensely the itchy sites of the bites, but in due course I became immune to these fascinating little insects and nowadays I am not usually aware of their presence until someone else insists on shooing them away. If you do not like mosquitoes they will drive you absolutely potty and one sometimes sees white visitors to the area flapping constantly at their attendant cloud of mossies. It does not do any good, of course, and you will always get fed up before the mosquitoes do.

The mosquitoes, however, are the only animals that are going to attack you. Contrary to popular belief you are not going to be instantly filleted by piranha if you jump into a river, though you should treat these fierce little fish with caution, nor is a jaguar going to leap on you from a tree. Few people are lucky enough to see one of these lovely cats in the wild. Really the only other beasts that might trouble you are jiggers, which are small invertebrates which lay their eggs on bare feet. When the larva hatches, which it does very fast in this highly competitive society (it is a real jungle out there!), it burrows beneath the skin and sits, just growing. Other insects leave their larvae beneath your skin as well and some of these can eventually reach the size of a cocktail sausage. It is not at all uncommon to come across animals infested with the things—baby birds especially. One can see the larvae moving about beneath the skin, and through a small hole at one end of its nursery you can actually spot the end of the insect. If you are unfortunate enough to become infested it is best to get rid of them as soon as you can as they are exceptionally uncomfortable. This is most efficiently done with something like a pin to enlarge the hole so that the maggot can be pulled out, after which the injury can be disinfected.

Occasionally you might find a few leeches on your legs though I have not had this happen in jungle, but rather in the waterways around the savannahs that sometimes border the forests. One of the most unpleasant of the Amazonian fauna with which to be infected is an incredible little fish known as the candiru, which enters the urethra or the anus, from which it is very difficult to dislodge it as the spines act as barbs to keep it in place. Candiru are really interesting as they are known to actually travel up a stream of urine to find a suitable orifice. Fortunately I have never encountered these little animals, but they do not sound much fun.

Apart from these you are safe, though there are a few stinging wasp-like insects that will have a go at you if you

Waorani settlement in Ecuador—the Waorani traditionally live away from rivers (*Adrian Warren*)
■

The Straits Times of Singapore has reported that in December 1987 an expedition to an area of rainforest in the Trus Madi range of hills in Tambunan in the Malaysian territory of Sabah discovered a new sub-species of *Rafflesia*, the world's largest flower. This particular one measured 9 in (23 cm) in diameter, the record for the species is about 3 ft (1 m).

This hitherto unknown sub-species has been named *Rafflesia tenfgku adlini* after the deputy director of the Sabah Foundation in recognition of his contribution to conservation. The leader of the expedition that found the plant, botanist Karamudin Mat Salleh, discovered the flower within the boundaries of a logging concession.

disturb their beautifully crafted homes, hidden beneath conveniently large leaves, and there are also some beautiful, large biting flies that give one of the most excruciating bites I have ever come across. But all these things happen only rarely and one can go for months without being bitten or stung.

Bearing all this in mind you can explore the site of the old village in which you find yourself, and enjoy the experience, for the area is sure to be rich in species. There will certainly be butterflies, and if the season is right these might be present in huge numbers. If the huts are still standing they are sure to provide you with all sorts of goodies. There will inevitably be small lizards scuttling about; ameivas on the ground, geckoes in the thatch, and brightly enamelled baby green iguanas everywhere. The whole place ought to be rich in insect species

Iguanas are common lizards throughout tropical America. Unlike other lizards, they are almost entirely vegetarian. They are strong swimmers, lay eggs which hatch into babies like this one, and are highly regarded as food by the people of the area (*Adrian Warren*)

(OPPOSITE)
Bird eating spiders are found in rainforests everywhere. They may look ferocious but most are placid and the effects of their bites are vastly overrated in literature. They mainly feed on invertebrates (*Peter Tryuk/ The Tropical Butterfly Garden*)

■

and if you spend a night in the place and use a Tilley lamp, you will almost certainly find several large and impressive beetles blundering into the glass cover.

Hunt around and without doubt you will discover a good crop of spiders. Some of the orb-web spiders, the ones that make what is conventionally thought of as a spider's web, that is to say a sort of wheel-shaped web, can be fairly large and beautifully marked, often in gold. It is rare to find real gold in nature. Usually it is yellow, but Mrs Wilson's tanager, a beautiful little bird from central and south America, has a gold head, some beetles are gold, and a few of these South American orb web spiders have gold abdomens. Have a look beneath the floor of the huts if they are raised, or else lift any bits of litter that may be left lying around and you will find some large bird-eating spiders, or as they are known in America, tarantulas. (Real tarantulas are nondescript little beasts that live in southern Europe.) Some of these spiders are superb animals. The largest of them all is the goliath bird-eating spider, a handsome brown, furry animal that can be found in pockets over the northern part of the continent. They are so large that if you keep one in a glass tank and the room is quiet you can actually hear the sound of their footsteps as they run across the glass. The commonest of the bird-eating spiders are little black ones, sometimes with pink-furred toes or handsome red-and-black-striped abdomens. None of them will do you any harm at all if you leave them alone.

If you scratch about searching for animals you might also be lucky enough to come across a snake or two, and, although some of the snakes of the area are venomous, most are not, but in any case, like the spiders, they are not going to hurt you if you do not disturb them. Almost certainly there will be scorpions around. Somehow one expects scorpions from somewhere like the Amazon rainforest to be large ferocious-looking black things, but in fact they are all small and easily overlooked.

Examine any holes you come across. Holes in the ground are particularly rewarding as they often seem to be shared by more than one occupant. I came across one in Guyana on one occasion that housed both a bird-eating spider and a toad, of all things. Toads and other amphibians should be everywhere, though the best time to find them is at night especially just after a downpour. In some places the din at times like this is such that it is difficult to hear conversation. Some amphibians are most accommodating and sit around where they can easily be seen, but many of the tiny tree frogs are extraordinarily difficult to find. They are usually tiny, frequently green or brown, and often on the other side of a leaf, whichever side of it you are. Talking of noise, when the amphibians are not making a din the

The quetzal is a magnificent bird of the Trogon family that inhabits the hilly rainforests from Mexico to Costa Rica at altitudes of up to 9000 ft (2743 m). The male measures a metre from the tip of the bill to the end of the long tail plumes. Clothed in red, blue and green feathers, the breathtaking beauty of this bird endeared it to the Aztecs and Mayas who revered it as the god of the air, and illustrations of it can be seen in their art. They never killed it, and though they used the long tail plumes for ceremonial purposes they always released the bird after extracting them.

Today it is the national symbol of Guatemala and appears on that country's postage stamps and coins; in fact, the currency of the country is a quetzal. But like most rainforest species the bird is becoming rarer as its forest home is destroyed.

forms of life as there is in a tropical rainforest. A very few seemingly identical acres of rainforest can support more species of tree than can be found throughout the whole of Europe, and it is not uncommon to find two hundred species of tree in a single hectare (about $2\frac{1}{2}$ acres).

As with the forests of South America, it is easier to hear animals in the jungles of the Far East than to see them, but having said that they are easier to spot in Asia, though again it is the smaller animals that are observed most readily. Butterflies can be seen in abundance, especially along the banks of rivers which penetrate the forest. Sometimes whole drifts of these animals may be seen resting beside the water, probing the mud with their delicate proboscises. Sit for a while in the jungle and you will soon hear the rustle of lizards in the undergrowth. They can be met with frequently, but only if one is willing to be patient since they all disappear at the slightest sound. Monkeys

One in every four medicines contains compounds that were originally derived from rainforest species.

and other small mammals such as tree shrews can be spotted without too much trouble, and if you know what you are looking for you can come across squirrels of different species, though they can be infuriating to watch because as soon as they become aware of you they scuttle to the other side of the tree trunk and peer carefully round at you. If you try and encircle the tree they will always keep on the side furthest from you until their nerve breaks and they disappear completely.

Climbing plants such as lianas and rattans are everywhere, and I find that for some reason one comes across plants in flower in Asian forest far more frequently than in south America, where, although there are plenty of epiphytic orchids and other plants in the trees, they rarely seem to flower. The fact that there are more flowering plants in Asian forests means that there is more fruit present and consequently more animal life to eat it. Birds are often spotted in a place like this, though to be honest what one sees is usually a brown flash from the corner of the eye, and when you turn your head there is no sign of life. Nevertheless there are tiny flowerpeckers to look at and gorgeous iridescent blue and black fairy bluebirds or vivid green fruitsuckers. A large, ripe pawpaw fruit is soon pulled to pieces by a host of small birds.

Westerners often feel threatened in a rainforest but it is a real pleasure to watch the people who live in them exploit their environment. I spent some time many years ago living with a family of animal catchers in a forest in Orissa in India. The village in which they lived seemed to be miles from anywhere, but that did not appear to present any sort of a problem. There were about a dozen huts in the village, all made from local trees. Virtually all the meat that was eaten in the village had been trapped by the hunters and, although whenever anybody did go to a town they would always bring back as much rice and lentils as they could carry, the remainder of what everyone ate was taken from the forest.

It was fascinating how much the villagers knew about natural history. They were superb and taught me much that I could not have learnt any other way. They taught me how to catch a wide variety of animals, what fruit was edible, how to make a sort of tea from some local rush-like plant and how to tap the sap of a palm tree to produce a slightly cloudy liquid to drink. First thing in the morning a pot of the stuff would be removed from the tree where it had been filling overnight, and the liquid would be strained through a threadbare bit of someone's dhoti to exclude all the bird faeces and the insects that had drowned in it. A glass full of the stuff would be offered to me. There is no more pleasing drink in the world. Nor was that the end of its usefulness because, if the liquid was

The sealing-wax palm, named after the colour at the top of the trunk (*Heather Angel*)

(OPPOSITE)
Harpy eagles are now rare in South America where they hunt over the treetops for the monkeys on which they feed (*Adrian Warren*)

An estimated 40,000 tigers lived in the forests of India at the turn of the century. Today the figure is about 4,000. In 1988 an Indian forestry officer broke up a country-wide ring involved in smuggling tiger bones to China and other places in Asia with large Chinese popula-tions. Three members of the gang were arrested and jailed under the 1972 Wildlife Preservation Act.

The officer responsible, V. M. Deshmukh, said that the group, which included seven women, had systematically trapped and killed tigers to salvage the bones which fetch high prices from Chinese pharmacists as an ingredient in medicine, and are said to cure backache. The tiger skins were sold to companies who made them into floor coverings and wall hangings. The members of the gang said that they had lost count of the number of animals they had killed, but that the demand was far higher than they could ever meet.

simply left to ferment all day in the heat, by the evening it had magically turned into a most potent alcoholic beverage that lubricated most satisfactorily many a friendly knees-up. Or again, if there was no intention to turn the stuff into toddy, it would be poured into a large shallow metal container rather like a giant wok and slowly boiled for a long time over an open fire. After many hours and much stirring the liquid first became a dark-brown syrup which could be used to add to food; when boiled even further it eventually became solid, rather like hard fudge. This was moulded into saucer-shaped cakes which could be used as sweets or in place of sugar or, better still, taken to the nearest bazaar where it could be sold. One can only eat a tiny scrap of the stuff as it is very sweet and has rather a strong taste, but it is much thought of in that part of the world.

I thoroughly enjoyed my time in that village except for the fact that whenever anybody wanted to defecate they would simply step into the jungle and do so. There was no sort of system to it or communal lavatory. Consequently one was never sure where to put a foot without stepping into human faeces, and the only place where you could be sure there would be none was in the middle of the paths to and from the village. That was fine for the villagers who simply came and went along the paths, but I was forever exploring the surroundings, looking for birds or flowers, or searching for spiders. I seemed to spend half my time cleaning my shoes, much to the amusement of the locals.

INDONESIA TO MADAGASCAR

Indonesian rainforest seems to be very green and lush, somehow, more so than the other forests of Asia. I am not sure that it really is, and one of the reasons that makes it appear so is that many of the plants seem to have larger leaves than those in other parts of the same region. It is very beautiful and often comes right to the edge of cultivated land, which in Indonesia is often in the form of terraced rice paddies. Consequently a constant background to the Indonesians working in their fields is the thick fringe of jungle.

Even though rainforest everywhere is disappearing fast, most of the islands between Singapore and Australia have some rainforest, and many of them are still covered in it.

Rainforests in Africa and some of its islands have a completely different nature again. The trees are different, the animals are different and the whole place has a feel that is unlike that in forests anywhere else. Even today expeditions are finding new species of plants and animals, which does not seem surprising when one looks at these and sees that most of them are fairly small, but it comes as a surprise to discover that it is only about a century since the okapi was first found in the

The pitcher plant traps insects to absorb their nutrients. This one was found on the Brunei/Sarawak border at an altitude of 4000 ft (*Adrian Warren*)

■

jungles of east Africa, and okapis are enormous animals that look rather like reddish-brown giraffes with short necks and the back legs of a zebra.

Africa has always held a fascination for many people, and for a long time it was known as the Dark Continent. Even today, surprisingly, many people think that the place is covered with forest from one end to the other. That is not so, of course, as today the jungle is confined to western Africa, though it stretches quite a way east. The filmmaker Armand Denis did not do much to extend his viewers' knowledge about the place. If you have ever seen any of his early films shot in that part of the world you can only wonder that anyone at all took them seriously at the time, but just after World War II the world was a far less sophisticated place and television was only in its infancy, and anything that appeared on it was assumed to be the truth. We now know that some of the sequences in those early films were pure fabrication.

Since white men first went to Africa and saw the forests for themselves, they have brought back stories of gorillas that persist to this day even in the face of contradictory scientific knowledge. One still hears stories of gorillas bearing screaming maidens into the jungle and pulling the heads off over-bold hunters. Only a year or two ago there was a lovely story in one

of the papers from that part of the world that told of a woman who was returning to her home after a day's work somewhere along a path through the jungle. On the way she felt tired so she sat down against the base of a tree and fell asleep. She was awakened by a large male gorilla that was busy raping her. She apparently screamed but the gorilla took no notice. Afterwards the gorilla disappeared into the trees leaving the woman in a considerable state of shock. However, before she could pull herself together and set off back to her village, the gorilla returned and repeated his rape of the poor woman. Eventually she did return home and, sobbing, told her husband what had happened. He apparently became very angry and accused her of tempting the gorilla, and colluding in the rape. The piece ended with the information that as a result of the happening the man was divorcing his wife for infidelity. The whole story was reported as fact, and apparently it was accepted and believed, as told, by all the people of the village involved. The story was shown to me by a chap who worked in an office in a large town in that part of the world. He found my incredulity very hard to accept. That sort of story still persists about gorillas, and for that matter some other apes.

There are bits and pieces of forest in other places but they are not likely to survive in a viable size for much longer. Much of Madagascar's forest has disappeared, and so has a lot of that in Vietnam, destroyed by an act of appalling vandalism by the American military during the Vietnam war when they sprayed the jungle with the defoliant Agent Orange.

ANIMAL RECORDS

I said earlier that rainforests provide a host of mind-boggling statistics and records. There is little point ploughing through all the statistics here as nothing is more boring than table after table of facts, but it is interesting to look through the records that are available. In 1979 zoologists found that the Bali leopard exists on that island, the first time there has ever been a record of the animal, which is regarded now as one of the world's rarest. The record for the world's slowest-moving land animal is held by the two-toed sloth from the rainforests of America. Kitti's hog-nosed bat caused considerable excitement when it was discovered some time ago. It is the lightest mammal in the world at around 2 g.

The rarest reptile in the world is said to be the Madagascar dwarf chameleon, and the world's heaviest snake is the anaconda, which can weigh nearly 500 lb (230 kg). Some people may feel this is surprisingly little, given the travellers' tales that turn up from time to time about snakes of colossal size. Though the reticulate python of south-east Asia has the record for the

Since 1945 over 40 per cent of tropical rainforests have disappeared forever, and as a result over 50 species of plants and animals become extinct every day.

Many of the arrow-poison frogs of the New World are vividly coloured. This one is carrying some of its tadpoles on its back (*Adrian Warren*)

(OPPOSITE)
Bats attract a bad press, but they are extraordinarily interesting animals. These are the fascinating little tent making bats from Costa Rica (*Adrian Warren*)

In 1989 the Australian prime minister announced that the country was going to replace a billion trees over the next ten years. The project would involve planting 273,972 trees a day!

longest snake, the aquatic anaconda is far more bulky. Everyone loves tales of venomous animals, and another Asian forest reptile species, the legendary king cobra, is without any doubt the longest venomous snake. It is quite thought-provoking to meet one of these handsome animals for the first time in the wild and to find that instead of standing up a matter of a few inches, as do most snakes, these beasts are another matter entirely. A common boa constrictor holds the record for longevity among snakes. One specimen is known to have lived over forty years.

Arrow poison frogs are super little animals, and one species from Cuba is the record-holder for the smallest amphibian, being only about a centimetre (less than half an inch) long. As if that were not enough, one species, the golden arrow poison frog, has the most active poison known to man, or at any rate so it is claimed, though people are always disputing facts like that.

The heaviest spider in the world was found in Brazil and weighed nearly 3 oz (85 g), while the largest was also found in that country. It measured nearly 11 in (28 cm) across. Both the heaviest and the largest insects are rainforest species. The $3\frac{1}{2}$ oz (100 g) goliath beetle is from west Africa, while Indonesia yields a 13 in (33 cm) long stick insect. One of the rarest insects of the world was found in Costa Rica: only two specimens of the butterfly known as the eight-spotted skipper have ever been discovered.

One of the shortest gestation periods in the animal world belongs to the yapok from the rainforests of the New World, while the remarkable thing about tenrecs, animals from Madagascar and Mauritius, is that one was discovered with the largest litter of babies known to have been born to a wild mammal, and in another species the female can breed about three weeks after birth.

Many bats live in tropical rainforests, and one of them, a fruit bat, has a wingspan about equal to your height, and we have already mentioned Kitti's hog-nosed bat as being the smallest.

Among rainforest primates there are a host of interesting records. Gorillas are the largest of all, while the forests of Indonesia house the smallest, the pen-tailed shrew. The rarest primate, the hairy-eared dwarf lemur, is from Madagascar, and it is said that chimpanzees are the strongest known primates though I have a feeling this might simply be because more research has been done with these animals than with any comparable ones. Though it must be said that they are extraordinarily strong, something the layperson tends to forget, seeing them only as a cross between cuddly toys and the stars of an advertisement for tea bags, but recently one pulled the arm right off a boy in a zoo in Britain.

Forests often start along the banks of rivers, since here they are able to obtain water and nutrients essential for growth. In time the new trees drop seeds which grow and the forest begins to expand (*Adrian Warren*)

The smallest deer come from the forests of Indonesia, and the rarest, Fea's muntjac, is only found in Thailand and Burma. Even the world of rainforest birds produces its records since the white-fronted falconet is a minute, sparrow-sized bird of prey from Borneo. Parrots are well-known as being long-lived birds, and two or three of the Amazon parrots and the Indonesian cockatoos can claim records in this area.

There are plenty of other animal records that relate to rainforest, covering just about any group of animals you care to mention, but the similar details for plants are every bit as fascinating. The largest flower in the world is the huge and flamboyant bloom of the corpse lily, so called because of the dreadful stink of putrefaction that it gives off. For all that, it is a handsome thing and comes from the forests of the Far East. The largest orchid comes from Malaysia and has petals 18 in (45 cm) long, and while we are in that part of the world it is as well to mention the fastest-growing tree in the world which reached an astonishing 35 ft (10 m) in thirteen months. It was also in this area that a tree managed to reach an astonishing height of 100 ft (30 m) in just over five years.

The whole world of the rainforest is extraordinary and of vital importance to the world generally, but even today with all the publicity it receives most people are ignorant of how important it is that we save it.

MOVING WITH THE TIMES

The Amerindians are having to become specialists in the art of communications and public relations these days, and it is not uncommon today to find one of them shooting pictures of a protest meeting with a video camera. Some of them have always been more ready than others to move with the times. Some years ago I was staying with a friend just outside Cayenne, the capital of French Guiana on the north-east coast of south America. The northern part of the country is marsh and savannah, but not far inland is the edge of the jungle. This particular friend had all sorts of small businesses in the area and one of them was a canoe safari business. It did not do too well because the country has not yet been discovered by tourists, thank goodness. Nevertheless a few of them find it, and Francis would wait until he had a good canoe load and arrange a day trip so that his customers could travel into the interior to visit a genuine Indian village. They loved it, but to see the whole thing from behind the scenes was vastly amusing. One day when Francis knew he would be taking a load of tourists he would call up the chief of his particular village on a short-wave radio that lived in the corner of Francis' bedroom. He would arrange a time, and in due course would deliver his tourists to the village for an hour or two of

Hummingbirds are commonly thought to be very tiny, but some species are comparatively large. The bee hummingbird is about the size of a bumble bee. The giant hummingbird, on the other hand, is over 8 in (20 cm) long.

Hummingbirds feed on nectar from flowers and on small flying insects. A bird will hover in front of a flower while it feeds, and these birds are the only ones with the ability to fly backwards. When hovering their wings beat around 55 times per second, but during courtship flights this rate can rise to 200 beats per second. Not surprisingly, the energy required for these feats means that the birds have to feed constantly throughout the day. Physiologists have proved scientifically that hummingbirds are incapable of long, sustained flight, but some hummingbirds, unaware of this research, continue to migrate distances of 500 miles (800 km), much of it across the sea.

Conservation is becoming increasingly important to Australians and is having a strong and probably permanent influence on Australian politics. Even the notoriously anti-conservation premier of Tasmania, Robin Gray, had to admit that this was so, when the conservation vote caused a swing away from his party. A Labour member of parliament campaigning on a conservation ticket, against the state's policy of destroying the rainforest, was elected to the federal House of Representatives for the first time in 12 years.

There are now several green candidates in the House, and a case is continuing in the High Court between the federal government and the government of the state of Tasmania about the continued destruction of forest for wood chipping in and around protected forest areas.

carefully choreographed photograph taking, after which they would all happily return to Cayenne. As soon as they had gone all the Indians (and they were real Indians) would leave their show village by a back trail through the jungle to their real village a quarter of a mile away. There they would wash off their paint, carefully put away their noble savage regalia and replace the jeans and T-shirts they had left off earlier in the day. Then they would pull cans of Kronenberg lager from their fridges and relax with a sigh in front of their radios. Later in the week one could see the most senior of the men in the capital where they would collect their wages from Francis, bank them and then visit the local Prisunic supermarket to stock up with food until the next time.

The whole business worked very well and everyone was happy. I cannot even find it in me to condemn the practice since these Indians were used to meeting foreigners. So often when people from another part of the world arrive in a primitive village they take with them a variety of illnesses to which they are immune. The poor villagers however have never come in contact with the illnesses before and, as a result, what to us are a mere nuisance can be life-threatening illnesses to them, and on more than one occasion villages have been wiped out on being infected with things like the common cold. Some countries are very aware of their responsibility to these less sophisticated citizens, and take care of them. French Guiana is one such and, apart from 'tame' Indians like this, it is very difficult for visitors to the country to obtain permits to visit areas in which the more distant tribes live. I was lucky enough to do so once and had a marvellous time. I even got shot by an arrow, which is always good as a talking point, even though the incident was not nearly as dramatic as it sounds. What happened was that I was standing in the village with one foot propped up on a fallen log when an agouti, a large forest-dwelling rodent rushed out between my feet. As an immediate reaction to seeing a piece of food suddenly disappear, one of the men took a shot at it, and as the arrow went past me it just grazed the skin of my ankle. I have had a worse scratch from my daughter's cat, but don't tell anyone!

On the other side of the world in Thailand, there is a delightful lady, Katy Buri, who cares desperately about the state of her country and gets really upset when she sees how the forest is being destroyed. So much so that she has bought a fruit farm right out in the middle of the country, next door to a piece of real rainforest, part of which is included in her land. She spends much of her time buying animals from the dreadful conditions they have to suffer in the markets and trying to keep them alive. When they recover she releases them on this patch of land,

This South American is still using a stone-headed axe to chop down a tree (*Adrian Warren*)

In 1987 42 people in Sarawak, a part of Malaysia on the island of Borneo, were arrested for having set up barriers in protest against the destruction of the forest. One of them, Harrison Ngau, was held for two months without trial, and has been under house arrest ever since. He was not allowed to leave Malaysia to receive a Right To Livelihood Foundation award at the British House of Commons in December 1988.

though she is uncomfortable about doing so, since, as she says, while they have been with her they have lost some of their fear of man, and without that they are open to being shot or recaptured. 'But what else can I do?' she asks plaintively. When last I saw her she was designing an aviary which she was going to construct right across her patch of rainforest. The cost was astronomical, and it is a good job she can afford it, but when it is done she will be able to release her orphans into the safety of this enclosure. She is especially interested in otters and hornbills, and it was with the latter in mind that she first conceived the idea. As it is, her large garden in Bangkok has become filled up with a number of otter enclosures. She has so many otter births these days that she refers to the babies as her crop.

For any number of reasons, rainforests are fascinating places and need to be saved now before it is too late to do anything about them. There are all sorts of unique plants and animals that we cannot do without.

WHAT IS A RAINFOREST?

A RAINFOREST IS AN extraordinarily complicated structure put together from innumerable elements that all work together. A gap in this system anywhere can cause a breakdown of the whole business.

We have already seen that at ground level there is not much light and as a result there can be little undergrowth. Nonetheless all sorts of things are happening at this level, just as they are elsewhere, but the level at which most things happen is without doubt right at the top of the trees. This part of the forest is known as the canopy and is as busy as New York or London.

However, the base of the forest, literally and metaphorically, is the soil upon which everything grows. Everywhere where there are rainforests one discovers that the earth is red, very sandy and of poor quality, containing few nutrients, which is why the growing of crops in these parts of the world is such a futile pastime. On top of this soil is a thin layer of humus, compost if you like, manufactured from the dead bodies of millions of trees and other plants, and animals. Leaves fall to the ground, trees topple and animals die. Very quickly their remains are broken down by a limitless army of organisms. Animals of all sorts soon start to eat any such food that comes their way, and beetles, ants, termites and other insects munch their way through any that might remain. At first it seems strange that a forest floor does not smell dank and rotten, but this is because everything is broken down so fast. Kick a horizontal tree trunk and the chances are that it will fall to pieces because the whole thing is riddled with the tunnels of termites that have reduced the tree to sawdust. Animals in this environment can fall prey to an infection of some sort early one morning and be dead by evening, so fast is the rate at which life is lived in these almost ideal conditions.

The Indonesian forests are made up of an enormous variety of elements. The trees of each species are usually found singly (*Adrian Warren*)

■

It is estimated that 25 million acres (10 million hectares) of Brazilian forest are destroyed annually, and, as a result, 31 species of the country's parrots are endangered.

All living plants and animals require three things to survive—food, moisture and warmth—and these are supplied in abundance in a rainforest, so within an hour anything dead is well on the way to being broken down. Fungi quickly begin to aid the process and bacteria are hard at work so that a week after an organism dies there is usually nothing to see of it, unless it is a large tree. The result of all this activity is a warm, brown, pleasant-smelling compost interspersed with leaf litter, seeds and much other debris, and it is in this layer of soil that all the plants grow. It is difficult to appreciate just how thin this layer is—only a few inches deep. Since it supports such a fertile structure above it one tends to assume that it is substantial, and this is the problem when even a small part of the forest is destroyed. As soon as it rains (and you do not know the

> **Despite Margaret Thatcher's alleged conversion to conservation, in July 1989 *The Sunday Times* revealed that Brazilian mahogany was to be used to embellish two rooms at 10 Downing Street.**

meaning of rain until you see a tropical downpour!) this thin, fragile topsoil is washed away into the nearest river. Most of the forest plants start their lives as seeds in this compost, seeds that have been released from parent plants high above, or from the faeces of birds that might have eaten the fruit containing them some distance away.

Very few seeds manage to produce mature plants. Many are eaten by agoutis, weevils or other floor-dwelling animals and those that do survive to germinate and root themselves successfully have still to grow in the face of enormous competition and pressure. The leaves of any plant are devoured avidly by all sorts of animals, and to combat this a number of plant species have developed toxins to prevent this happening. Others protect themselves with spines and thorns, and some have attendant colonies of ants that live within their tissues and charge out to repel any predatory insect that attempts to eat the leaves. Small plants have an awful struggle to survive anyway since the light levels are so low that they cannot photosynthesise properly. Some species overcome this by trailing along the ground until they find a large, successful tree, and they use this as a support to climb towards the light hundreds of feet above. Others simply have to stay alive as best they can until a nearby tree dies and crashes to the ground, leaving a valuable hole of sunlight in the otherwise impenetrable canopy. When this happens every plant at the bottom of the hole puts on growth very rapidly, but, even so, only the very strongest plants will make it to the sunlight.

A mature tree then flowers and bears seeds that in turn drop to the forest floor. In the meantime it becomes the host to other plants like the climbers we mentioned a moment ago, but in addition every adult tree in the forest is festooned with a variety of smaller plants. Each hollow at the junction of branches and in the bark soon bears small ferns, cacti, orchids or some

While many flowers are happy to be fertilised by any suitable agent that comes along, others have developed specifically to attract particular animals. Hummingbirds are responsible for fertilising many plants, and flowers have evolved so that pollen is brushed onto the heads of birds coming to feed on the nectar (*Brian Rogers/Biofotos*)

(OPPOSITE)
Weevils are essential for the breakdown of dead timber. This pair from Malaysia appear flamboyant, but in the wild are very difficult to see (*Peter Tryuk/The Tropical Butterfly Garden*)

sort of plant. In the New World forests, the trees also support a host of bromeliads. Most of them have a rosette of leaves which have a hollow 'vase' in the centre. This vase is filled with water and in time becomes a home to a variety of animals. Some tree frogs spend their entire lives in these bromeliads, laying their eggs in the vase, where the minute tadpoles grow and from where they eventually climb out onto the leaves. The water in the centre of the plants drips from other plants and contains many nutrients that the bromeliad extracts for its own use. One species of bromeliad is known as Spanish moss. It gives some American rainforests a very typical appearance. The plant hangs in great grey swathes from the branches of the trees, imparting an atmosphere typical to this type of forest.

Many of the plants that have become popular as house plants in Europe and America started life in rainforests. *Tillandias* are bromeliads, and are sold in shops as air plants, and a whole lot of other creeping, trailing plants from the jungle also decorate our homes.

The trees themselves and many of the plants that live on them provide homes for animals that have developed to exploit not the forest floor but one of the environments found above it. In the region between the floor and the canopy one finds a whole lot of interesting invertebrate fauna together with species that like living in holes in trees. A tree whose heart has rotted

Only 1–2 per cent of light at the top of a rainforest canopy manages to reach the floor below, and the wavelengths of this remaining light are such that it is useless for photosynthesis.

and is slowly dying provides hollow interiors of trunk or branches, which form the residences of squirrels, birds, insects and spiders, but it is not until you emerge into the canopy that the full extent of the range of animal species hits you.

An Indian in Ecuador climbs high into the forest canopy, which is rich in animal and plant life absent from the jungle floor (*Adrian Warren*)
■

FROM CANOPY TO RIVERBED

For a very long time man had not managed to penetrate this part of the forest and so only received tantalising glimpses from below of what went on amongst the leaves. Then, as so often happens, several people at once began to make forays into this region. Some years ago a young British film-maker, Phil Agland, wanted to make a programme about the roof of the rainforest in west Africa. He laboriously climbed to the top of a tree and built himself a ramshackle, Robinson Crusoe hut, and apart from brief forays to the ground he lived in this precarious home for the next several years, extending it outwards with rickety walkways. The result was the best rainforest film anywhere, *Korup*. It was the transmission of that film that really started off the current interest in the jungles of the world. It went on to win awards and led to the setting up of a conservation programme to save Korup from destruction.

Also about this time the British broadcaster David Attenborough was presenting a series of programmes on television about just about every group of plants and animals. The series was known as *Life on Earth*, and for it a brief sequence was shot during which David was hauled up a tree in a rainforest on the end of a system of ropes and pulleys so that he could demonstrate the different levels as one travelled between the ground and the canopy. But it was really a fellow countryman who started to look at the canopy seriously. Andrew Mitchell and his colleagues built accommodation at the top of a tree in Amazonia and extended it with a far more sophisticated network of aerial roadways than Phil Agland had ever dreamed of. Andrew and his friends spent a lot of time researching what they found in the canopy and he afterwards wrote a book called *The Enchanted Canopy* which tells the story of the enterprise. It was well worth all the effort. As he says, fear of falling had kept most humans firmly within a few feet of the ground throughout millions of years, and when they finally reached the top Andrew and his party discovered things that had never been thought of before.

There had been other attempts at climbing into the canopy of course, but they had been comparatively primitive affairs, and some of them were decidedly eccentric. One American, Elliott McClure, got to the top of his tree in Malaysia up a ladder, which must have been a frightening experience (so much more convenient to ascend in an armchair attached to pulleys!).

Britain imported more tropical hardwood in 1984 than any other country except Japan. Whereas it is possible to argue for the use of a few rainforest timbers, there are perfectly suitable alternatives for virtually everything made from them. Coffins are frequently made from tropical hardwoods, and these are either burnt or buried for ever at the funeral. For centuries British boatbuilders proudly built craft from native hardwoods, but today the industry uses tropical timbers as well.

It is the canopy which makes the forest work, for it is here that the trees can photosynthesise in the sunlight, without which they would not survive. This means that to the human being in the canopy there is a continuous carpet of leaves and flowers, fruit and seeds. These in turn attract a wealth of wildlife which feeds on the vegetation, and in turn other animals are attracted to the area to prey on the first lot of animals. Consequently it is this part of the forest that is the busiest of all, but it ought not to be forgotten that another very important part of the system is to be found far below in the waterways that run through the forest.

The wider rivers are much like rivers anywhere, opaque and a sort of muddy khaki unless they are reflecting the blue sky, but the smaller creeks are extraordinary places. Many of them are fairly narrow, not more than a very few feet across, but they can be frighteningly deep, and crossing them via a fallen log which perhaps has been worn smooth by generations of bare feet is a worrying process. A funny thing about the water in rainforests is the variety of colours. Some can be almost white and in other places just as black. Where the River Negro joins the Amazon the two colours are especially obvious, and for quite a distance the two streams of water run alongside each other until they merge into a generally dirty colour, but before they do there is a distinct and obvious line between the two. Red water is common too. It is highly acidic and if you swim in it your eyes soon begin to sting. The red water can be as clear as crystal, and looking down through it one can see a formidable tangle of roots and fallen branches at the bottom.

The very deep, very clear streams appear to harbour little in the way of living organisms, but in the shallower, less coloured water there are all sorts of things. Peering down through the surface one sees fish of a million species, though few of them are more than the length of a finger. On occasion though, the slow, long shape of an electric eel can be watched drifting through the black roots. The ones I have seen are a very dark brown with a red fringe to the ventral fin. I know it is an anthropomorphic observation, but the deliberate, confident advance of one of these fish through the water seems full of menace. Perhaps I am biased after accidentally treading on one when I was wading through a marsh which was full of the things. That is not a fun experience and definitely to be avoided especially as a large, healthy eel can generate a current of up to 600 V. I am sure these fish are no more full of menace than any other animal, and I daresay they can feel good humoured like the rest of us, but they look dangerous!

If you think that sounds silly, let me tell of a zoological friend of mine who did most of his national service in Malay. He

Most snakes are not venomous, nor in any way dangerous, but this fer de lance is a South American pit viper that can deliver a lethal bite from two fangs which fold away when not in use (*Adrian Warren*)

was particularly interested in snakes and kept quite a few in suitable containers in his mess hut. One day he was going on leave, and during his absence the rest of the unit was departing on exercise to another part of the country where Peter thought there might well be an interesting variety of serpents. He asked the friends who shared his billet if they would collect any that they came across while they were there, and keep them until he got back from leave. 'But be careful', he told them, 'to leave alone any venomous species you might come across'. Now, anyone who knows anything about snakes knows that there is no real way of telling whether a snake is venomous or not when you come across it in the wild, especially as all you usualy see is a tail disappearing beneath a bush. So if you do not know what the venomous snakes of an area look like, you cannot tell whether a particular snake you come across presents any danger. When Peter returned from his holiday he asked whether his colleagues had managed to collect any animals for him while he was away.

Oh yes, they said, they are in that box under the bed. Peter carefully opened the box and lovingly examined the new and marvellous additions to his collection and spent a few happy hours housing them. When he had finished he realised that there had not been a single venomous one amongst them and asked how the collectors had managed to differentiate. 'Oh, we left the poisonous ones alone,' he was told. He asked how they had know which was which. The answer was that the venomous ones had 'looked venomous'.

Occasionally a traveller comes across snakes swimming across the rivers and creeks in a forest, but that does not happen often. On one occasion I discovered several small holes in the sand alongside a stream. I asked the Indian I was with what they were, and he told me they were the holes of electric eels. When the water rose the holes were submerged and the eels came out into the river. Eels can certainly manage out of water for a considerable time and there are many stories of them travelling overland, sometimes for considerable distances. However my Indian insisted that the water entering the holes stimulated the eels to emerge. On that occasion, the first time I had been to the jungles of South America, I had taken a rubber dinghy for use on the rivers. I soon discovered that there could hardly be a more useless craft for exploring the smaller creeks as they were so full of sticks and roots that the bottom of the boat was constantly getting stuck, and on more than one occasion punctures appeared and the boat started to fill with water. The craft was more nuisance than it was worth and we abandoned it fairly soon. A canoe was far more sensible.

In these creeks, when it rains, the rain water settles at the top, and Indians showed me that when one wanted a drink one

Brazil heads the list of countries with the largest number of endangered bird species. At the last count it had 34 endangered species, but in the light of recent knowledge this may have to be amended to 150. There are over 10 species in the same situation throughout Asia and Australia and more than 20 in China.

There are thought to be less than 25 specimens of the Madagascar sea eagle in the wild as well as the Mauritius kestrel, parakeet and pink pigeon and the Puerto Rican parrot.

Despite the outrage from some conservationists who should know better, any hope of survival for many species of animals and plants lies only in their propagation in captivity. The Jersey Wildlife Preservation Trust specialises in endangered species, including the Mauritius pink pigeon, and some captive birds from the collection have been returned to their island home.

The seringueros, or rubber tappers of Brazil lead a hard life with little reward. They are up at dawn to wash in the nearby creek before setting off for the day's work (*Adrian Warren*)
■

restaurant, and perfectly content with his lot. To many it might not have seemed much of a life but, as he said, after you have spent thirty odd years in the penal establishment of Devil's Island, almost anything else is luxury. At least one ex-convict has done well for himself, opening and running an excellent restaurant in one of the small towns along the coast.

At almost any time one can find small camps of people trying to eke a living from the rainforests of the world. Sometimes they are panning for gold in the rivers, sometimes they are looking for precious stones. All of these people have arrived after hearing stories of marvellous riches found by someone else, and driven on by the belief that tomorrow will be the day when they will find a huge gold nugget or the biggest emerald ever. Many years ago in Ceylon I found two or three fairly valuable stones in the forest while looking most casually. I happened to be with a local friend who had alerted me to the presence in the area of gemstones, otherwise I would not have bothered to pick them up as I know nothing about the subject. I later took them to Paris where they brought me a few hundred pounds when a few hundred pounds was worth having.

Other people come to the forest too, and perhaps the most

interesting story is that of the South American rubber boom. The Indians of South America have always known about rubber, or balata as they called it, but when the developed world suddenly decided that it could not manage without the stuff, many thousand of people flocked to Brazil to cash in on the crop with the same fervour as the gold prospectors of the Yukon. The business was definitely worth while from a financial point of view and lots of people became very rich through it, though at the same time it must be said that the most awful things were done to the poor rubber tappers by their bosses who treated them dreadfully. The rubber boom resulted in small communities cropping up throughout the forest to tap the trees, collect the rubber and get it back to a port from which it could be shipped to other countries. Manaus, previously a collection of a few huts a thousand miles from the mouth of the Amazon River, suddenly became the centre of the trade and was turned into a thriving community with every facility possible. It even boasted an impressive opera house so that the rubber barons and their ladies could hear the latest stars of the opera world who were brought in to perform.

The business was vigorously protected but one day someone smuggled a few rubber tree seeds out of the country, or so the story goes. Another version has it that it was seedlings that were taken. Whichever it was they ended up in Malaya where they grew and flourished and became the beginning of a whole new way of life in that region, so much so that soon most of the world's rubber was coming from the Far East and Brazil's rubber industry collapsed. Fortunes were lost and much misery ensued. Today Manaus is a strange place. It is a busy port, though parts of it are very run down, but other parts are active and cared for, and the opera house is still there. When last I visited the place a number of years ago one could still see the sad and faded glory of what must have been a super building at one time, inhabited by many small animals and completely unused by humans.

Some rubber is still produced in Brazil, and quantities of the stuff are exported from the Far East, but today more and more synthetics are being used to replace the original product, and the forests are now being exploited in a completely different fashion from the way they were in the days of the rubber boom.

A rainforest, then, is an extraordinarily complicated world where every part is closely related to every other part, and each depends on the other for the whole system to work. There is so much going on in a rainforest that even today the greater part of it has not been researched and very little is understood about it. Each bit has taken millions of years to evolve, and it is going to take a long time before we can make sense of all that happens in the forests.

Rubber is obtained by scoring a diagonal cut through the bark of a rubber tree and letting the white liquid latex trickle into a collecting cup. When that cut has stopped producing, a further cut is made next to it. Eventually the bark is covered in old scars (*Adrian Warren*)

∎

ANIMALS OF THE RAINFOREST

Contrary to popular belief, mountain gorillas are gentle animals, which prefer to be left alone. Each night they make night nests for themselves in the trees (*Adrian Warren*)

∎

The Indonesian government claims that 300 million acres (120 million hectares) of the country are forested, but that was also their figure for the 1960s, since when millions of tonnes of timber have been extracted.

AS WE HAVE ALREADY seen, rainforests are rich in animal species, and just about every group of animals has representatives in the forest. The only animals that are almost lacking are large mammals, though there are one or two. Perhaps the largest of all is the okapi, a shy, elusive beast from west Africa. There is also of course that best known of all animals, the gorilla.

There are two types of gorilla, so similar that it takes a specialist to tell them apart. They are confined to the African rainforest and Ruanda has taken on their protection in a big way. Tours are run to enable visitors to watch gorillas in the wild, and they prove to be very popular. The animals bring in a fair amount of foreign revenue and so they are carefully protected. John Burton of the Flora and Fauna Preservation Society was telling me some time ago how he came across small boys in that country selling the little wire toys that seem to be produced everywhere in Africa. One of the versions was of a man riding a tricycle, designed so that the rotation of the wheels made the rider's legs appear to be actually pedalling. John persuaded the local children that the toy ought to be adapted so that instead of a human rider the toys featured a gorilla. This was taken up with enthusiasm and now the children of the country are also aware that it is worth saving gorillas.

The other large apes, the orang-utan of the Far East and the chimpanzee, are all forest species, and are all fairly large. Chimps can grow as big as you or me, which is something that most people do not realise. Some of my favourite primates are gibbons, of which there are several species, again, like the orangs, from the Far East. Every one of the primates mentioned so far is protected, yet chimps, orangs and gibbons are all still traded. If you know where to go you can find baby animals

hidden away in animal dealers' compounds and in the dingier realms of animal markets. I was offered two orangs in the Indonesian town of Pontianak and various species of gibbons in all sorts of places throughout Indonesia, Malaysia and Thailand.

The red-faced uakari is one of the largest of the South American monkeys, many of which are small enough to be cupped in two hands (*Adrian Warren*)

■

THE MONKEYS

Smaller primates are also to be found in rainforests. There is a whole range of monkey species in the jungles of the Celebes, Indonesia, south-east Asia generally and India, where a real delight is to watch a troop of langurs swing through the trees. I cannot help feeling that rhesus monkeys are the thugs of the simian world, but I have a particular affection for langurs. Some of the monkeys of tropical Africa are delightful, and that continent has an extensive and varied monkey population, amongst them some of the most colourful of the world's monkeys. Most are fairly large, though there are smaller ones, like the little talapoin which are strange little bundles of green fur.

The forest monkeys of the Americas are varied and extraordinary. Some of them are fairly large and look like one imagines a monkey to look, but many species are very small, and in fact the tiniest monkey in the world, the pigmy marmoset, comes from this region. You could sit one in a breakfast cup with no trouble and still leave room for the milk and sugar. An interesting fact about the New World monkeys is that some of them have prehensile tails. It is a common misconception that this is true of monkeys generally but in reality the feature is only found in this region. A spider monkey can hang by its tail from a branch with no trouble while it picks leaves or fruit to eat. Some species look quite bizarre to the layperson and the red uakaris invariably invite comparison with bald old men since the whole head has no hair and the skin is bright red. Sakis are odd-looking beasts as well, but I feel that some of the most beautiful of all primates are the smaller species from Central and South America. Squirrel monkeys are exquisite little mites, though nowadays their numbers are declining fast as huge quantities have been exported for research.

Many of the tamarins and marmosets are singularly beautiful, and some of the most spectacular are the various golden lion tamarins, some of which are completely covered in a long, gold pelt. They are very rare these days and confined to a small part of the forest where they are strictly protected but, like the apes mentioned earlier, these also are captured and find their way into trade, though nowadays only in very small numbers. Nonetheless, the populations are so small that it is questionable whether even this can be tolerated any longer.

Emperor tamarins are about the same size as the other

The giant otter, whose range once took in most of South America, can now be found only in countries along the north western coast. It is supposed to be protected throughout its range, but hunting for its fur continues.

Giant otters are known as water dogs by the local people. The animals feed almost exclusively on fish, mostly cichlids. Wealthy sporting fishermen blame the otters for their poor catches of these fish. The otters have a flexible social organisation, dependent on the particular set of environmental conditions in which the animal finds itself.

Giant otters look very much like a large version of the animal most of us are familiar with, though they are far more vocal and often the first sign of their presence is their call, especially if there are hungry cubs around.

species, which is to say about the size of a good handful, and are clothed in black and reddish brown, and sport a long flowing moustache of white. When the first skins were received by taxidermists in Germany many years ago, the animals had not been observed in the wild by the people who were mounting the skins, so, making a wild guess and hoping no doubt for a bit of royal patronage, the taxidermists waxed these facial hairs and curled them up on each side of the animal's head in imitation of their beloved kaiser, thus earning the animal the name emperor tamarin.

One of my favourites among the small South American monkeys is the silvery marmoset. This has been so ever since I watched one at Jersey Zoo early one morning long before the visitors entered. This little animal had recently been fed and, together with the fruit and everything else, the keeper had thrown a small handful of mealworms onto the floor of the outdoor enclosure. One of the marmosets was standing on its hind legs in the grass keeping careful watch to see where the next mealworm would make an appearance between the leaves of the grass. It leant forward, hands outstretched, waiting patiently, and on seeing a movement would suddenly pounce. It was a funny and appealing cameo, and at that moment I fell in love with the animal.

THE GIANT MONKEY?

One of the most intriguing stories about primates from South America is that of the giant monkey. Some decades ago, I think in about 1925, an expedition in what was then British Guiana came across a giant monkey of a hitherto unknown species. Someone in the party shot it and there remains a poor-quality photograph showing the hunter, and as far as I remember one or two other people as well, standing beside the corpse which had been propped up in a sitting position on a stool. At a guess the monkey must have been something like 5 ft (1.5 m) high standing on its hind legs. For some reason no part of the body was saved and the only evidence that the whole thing happened is this single photograph. No other giant monkeys have been found since. I would guess from the look of it that the animal was some species of spider monkey but I would love to know what it really was.

Monkeys are not the only mammals to inhabit rainforests, or even the only mammals to inhabit the canopies. There are plenty of squirrels as well, and in south-east Asia there is an animal that looks just like a squirrel though it is not related to them in any way. It is called the tupaia, or sometimes the tree shrew, and is a primate; that is, it is a relation of monkeys, apes and humans.

The Amerindian word for jaguar, Jaguara, means 'He who strikes down his prey in a single bound', which is an excellent way of describing this, the largest feline in Latin America. The large, Old World cats kill their prey by biting the neck, but jaguars crunch straight through the skull.

Although the species enjoys complete protection throughout its range under Appendix I of CITES (the Convention on International Trade in Endangered Species), it is hunted extensively everywhere that it is to be found. The largest threat to the animal, however, is the loss of its habitat — the rainforest. Jaguar numbers are declining fast and it is already extinct in much of its former range; the only places where it can still be regarded as relatively common are the most remote parts of Belize and Guatemala.

Golden lion tamarins are extraordinary and breathtakingly beautiful little monkeys from South America, resembling little golden toys. They are one of the rarest primates in the world. It is unlikely that more than 150 survive in the wild, and those that do are restricted to the 5000 or so hectares of the Poco das Anas Biological Reserve in Brazil.

Golden lion tamarins, and their even rarer relative the golden rumped lion tamarin, are in theory protected, but it is still going to be hard work saving them from extinction. Fortunately they do well in zoos so that people have a chance to see these remarkable animals. The figures below are for 1984, the latest year for which they are readily available, though there is no doubt that all the listed collections have increased their stocks by now through breeding.

Jersey Wildlife Preservation Trust was the first European zoo to receive golden lion tamarins. It had six

The golden lion tamarin is very rare indeed and confined in the wild to a very small area of forest in Brazil (*Adrian Warren*)

■

adult and two infant pairs, one of the males coming from the Oklahoma Zoo. Sixteen have been reared, and six have gone to other zoos.

The London Zoological Society had two pairs, a single male and two as yet unsexed animals. One of the males arrived from Brookfield Zoo, Chicago, and a female came from Folsom Children's Zoo in the United States.

Belfast Zoological Gardens had two pairs, both of which have given birth to twins.

One male came from Tulsa, USA.

Howletts Zoo Park in Kent had a pair. They arrived in 1984, the female from Monkey Jungle, Florida.

Kilverstone Wildlife Park in Norfolk had two females and a male. One of the females is from Woodland Park Zoo, Seattle, and the other from Riverbank Zoo, Columbia, South Carolina.

Marwell Zoo Park had a pair. The male is from Los Angeles.

Paignton Zoological Gardens had three females.

Penscynor Wildlife Park had two pairs.

One female was from Tulsa and the other from Denver, Colorado. One male came from San Antonio, Texas.

Twycross Zoo had two females and a male. The females came from Monkey Jungle, Florida, and Los Angeles Zoo.

More information on the breeding of golden lion tamarins may be obtained from Elizabeth Yoshimi Nagagata or Lou Anne Dietz, Programma de Educacao Conservacionista, Projeto Micoleao Dourada, Reserva Biologica de Poco das Antas, Casimiro de Abreu, Rio de Janeiro, CEP 28 860, Brazil.

Ring-tailed lemurs are perhaps the best known of Madagascar's fauna. Less shy than many other lemurs, they spend longer on the ground where they are easy to observe (*Adrian Warren*)

∎

LEMUR TO LORIS

In a few parts of the world (eg, Madagascar) one can also come across those other delightful primates, the lemurs, which fill much the same ecological niche as the monkeys. Many people do not realise that there are many species of lemur and without doubt the best known is the attractive ring-tailed lemur, which has now been made into a delightful soft toy whose sales result in a small royalty going towards the animal's conservation.

One can accept that monkeys occur in the treetops—after all we are brought up with the image of monkeys swinging through the branches—but it comes as something of a surprise to see some of the other denizens of the trees. Of course in reality they are highly specialised forms that are perfectly adapted to life in the trees, but who would believe a tree kangaroo if someone came out with the idea halfway through a party? There is one, though, in the forests of Papua New Guinea. And who could invent a sloth, a slow-motion animal that lives its life hanging upside-down beneath the branches of trees and which has to come down to the ground to defecate? As though that is not crazy enough, everything else to do with the sloth is peculiar. The hair grows the wrong way so that there is a parting along the centre of its chest and stomach. Of course,

62

when you think about it the reason is obvious—the rainwater runs off—but it still sounds odd. The fur of a sloth is colonised by algae which give the animals a green tinge so that for all the world they look like the punks of the animal kingdom, and in this green fur live some small moths. The moths spend their lives on the sloth until it climbs down to the ground to defecate. When that happens the female moths run like mad, jump off, lay their eggs in the pellets of dung, and leap back on before their host disappears once again into the treetops!

The tamandua is another animal from the same region that I have an affection for. It is a small ginger teddy bear with a long nose that feeds on ants. It has a prehensile tail and, if you happen to be climbing a tree and come into close contact with it, it will stand upright on its back legs, holding on tightly with the tail and, reaching out with two front legs, it will have a go at you if you get too close. Tamanduas have jolly long claws and it is best not to tangle with one of them. None the less I feel they have a sort of cuddly appeal, though they are not as teddy like as some of the Old World rainforest mammals such as the agwantibo from west Africa or the bushbabies. Bushbabies have universal appeal with their short muzzles and huge eyes. The size of the eyes is to help them at night really, since they are nocturnal, rather than to make them look cuddly.

The bushbabies' place is taken in the Far East by the lorises, which are very like soft toys (though their limbs are longer and slimmer than most). Consequently they are captured and sold throughout the region as pets. However it needs a fair bit of experience to keep them properly and most of them die in captivity fairly soon. One of their requirements is a constant supply of live insects on which to feed, something that only the dedicated are willing to provide. They look sad little things in the tiny wire cages in which they are sold, though perhaps their fate is no less awful than the lorises in India whose eyes are removed for use in some folk medicine. The dreadful thing is that the eyes are removed from the living, conscious animal which is afterwards returned to the tree on which it was found. I was with some hunters one night, and asked them why they did it. The answer was that their religion forbade the taking of life.

BIRD LIFE

Perhaps it is the bird life of the rainforest that is the most spectacular and the most plentiful though much of it remains hidden from the ground. The appearance of birds in an area is seasonal, depending on the availability of food, so a tree coming into flower or the hint of ripening fruit will attract birds from miles around. At ground level the most you can expect to see are the herons and their cousins, which haunt every patch of

The chimpanzee is well-known as one of the few animals that uses tools. Only comparatively recently, however, has it been discovered by Mariko Hiraiwa-Hasegawa of Tokyo University, and Hiroyuki Takasaki and Richard and Jennifer Byrne of the University of St Andrews that chimps actually make attacks on predators. They have been observed stealing a three-month-old leopard cub from its mother and subsequently killing it by slapping, poking, and biting it and deliberately dropping it on the ground.

They were also seen on one occasion attacking an adult lion, though the animal took no notice of their attentions and in time they wandered off. Some years ago a stuffed leopard was placed in an area occupied by chimps so that their attitude to it could be filmed. When the leopard was discovered it was savagely attacked by the chimpanzees who used sticks to beat it with.

water they can find. Sometimes one also comes across kingfishers, which can be tiny and brightly coloured or fairly large birds, larger than one expects a kingfisher has any right to be.

In the Amazon region lives the hoatzin. If you set out to design a joke bird for a cartoon I suspect it would look much like a hoatzin, which is quite extraordinary. It nests in small trees over the banks of rivers, and can fly if it must, though it is almost as useless at it as I am at carpentry. When there are chicks in the nest and danger approaches, the babies will jump out and dive into the river below to swim away. They have small hooks on each wing to help them pull themselves up again.

Provided there are some flowers in bloom at ground level, and this sometimes occurs where a tree has fallen, or occasionally along a river, you might come across hummingbirds in Central and South America. Everyone thinks that all hummers are tiny, and it is true that many of them are, but the biggest, the giant hummingbird, is as big as a sparrow. The sword-billed hummingbird is fairly small, but it has a beak longer than itself. Beaks on hummers come in a wide variety of shapes, each designed to enable the owner to take nectar from flowers in the most efficient way. It is not true however that hummers feed only on nectar, since they all take considerable quantities of

A yellow oriole beside its nest at Apure in Venezuela. Surprisingly, though some forest birds are vividly coloured, they are often difficult to spot amongst the foliage until they move (*Adrian Warren*)
■

insects as part of their diet, and for this reason can sometimes be seen hawking above streams and rivers. It is sometimes difficult to appreciate the often multicoloured, highly iridescent plumage of these birds since the coloration is not caused by pigment but by refraction of the sun's rays. Often if the light source is not in the right direction a hummingbird can look black or nondescript brown.

Victorian and Edwardian zoologists and explorers used to name their discoveries far more adventurously than people do nowadays, and they were so impressed with the hummingbirds they met for the first time that they went wild with their nomenclature. There is one species named the fiery topaz and another called John's dagger (I wonder who John was). There is a whole group collectively known as hermits, and I have a scientific paper delightfully entitled *The Singing Assemblies of Hairy Hermits*—doesn't that conjure up some marvellous images?

Visitors to Africa or Asia frequently say they have seen hummingbirds but what they have confused with these American species are the sunbirds of the Old World. Some of these are also forest species and sometimes they can be found in large numbers where a tree is in flower. Despite their often flamboyant plumage they are surprisingly difficult to spot and it is often their nondescript but distinctive calls that alert one to their presence.

The extraordinary hoatzin lives along the rivers of South America. It builds its nest over water, and if the chicks drop into the river they can make their way ashore before pulling themselves back up using claws on the wings (*Adrian Warren*)

(LEFT)
A sifaka (pronounced shifark) and its baby in Madagascar, where the forests are fast disappearing beneath cattle and sisal plantations (*Adrian Warren*)
■

In south-eastern Brazil, forest destruction between Rio Grande do Sul and Bahia has meant that the original forest has now been cut up into a mosaic of separate bits and pieces. Consequently the 115 species of bird (94 of which are endemic) that live in this small area are now in considerable trouble. One of the rarest is the spix macaw, which comes from a restricted area. The local population is said to be very small, and there are only a few in captivity around the world where efforts to breed them are slowly proving successful. Macaws generally are having a hard time as

The South American blue-and-gold macaw that is now under threat due to the destruction of the forests (as indeed are all macaws) (*Adrian Warren*)

∎

the forest disappears. Large animals always survive less well than small species when their environment is endangered, and in addition macaws have to face the threat from bird catchers, since they are highly prized for their plumage.

Parrots galore inhabit the tropics and, although lots of them are not necessarily to be found in rainforests, some species, especially in South America and Indonesia, are very much forest birds. They are easier to spot than many, and their noisy calls are a sure clue to their presence. Sometimes they can be found in large numbers at a special place, either at a fruiting tree or, as I have seen in Central America, at a cliff which the birds scrape away with their powerful beaks to eat the soil, which must provide an essential nutrient of some sort. A huge flock of scarlet macaws at a feast like this has to be seen to be believed since macaws are coloured like a good day at playschool—every colour imaginable. On the other side of the world, in the Indonesian area, the large parrots are the cockatoos, which are mainly white, though their plumage is sometimes suffused with pink or yellow, a colour often duplicated in their crests. One or two of them are dark coloured, like the majestic black palm cockatoo, a bird that is rapidly becoming rarer through disappearance of its habitat and over-collection. Outside its own part of the world captive specimens are rarely seen, but it is so frequently encountered throughout the Far East in bird markets and shops that someone I knew once expressed surprise that it was rare and protected since there were so many freely on display. Despite the fact that they look large and well able to take care of themselves, black palm cockatoos are not easy to establish in captivity and the losses in the early days are high.

Small vividly coloured birds are legion throughout the rainforests of the world, and there are innumerable small brown ones that are indistinguishable in the wild. It is not until one is able to examine them closely that one comes to realise just how beautifully marked many of them are even though the tones of their plumage may be sombre.

TAPIRS TO MILLIPEDES

There is a host of ground-living mammals in this sort of environment. One of the most interesting is the tapir, because tapirs occur in two places; in South America, and right round the world in the forests of south-east Asia. They are very similar in appearance except for the colour, for the south American species are brown, while the Asian is black and white. At first sight they are strange-looking beasts, rather like giant pigs with a sawn-off elephant trunk in place of a more conventional nose. They are so odd that for a long time they have been regarded with a variety of emotions, and some time ago a writer, attempting to carry on Conan Doyle's adventures of the most famous fictional detective of all time, Sherlock Holmes, wrote a novel about a further adventure of his, entitled *The Giant Rat of Sumatra*. This turned out to be a tapir that was brought to

This puma kitten in Venezuela will lose its markings when adult. These attractive cats are no threat at all to human beings, but, like most forest cats, their numbers are decreasing (*Adrian Warren*)

■

Victorian London, escaped and went round the countryside savaging people. In fact tapirs are vegetarians, though they have fair old teeth and can bite like a champion. I used to know a chap who lost a kneecap to a tapir bite.

I said that tapirs look a bit like pigs, and so they do, but there are also real pigs inhabiting the floors of rainforests. Again in South America, the most common is a surprisingly small pig which stands only about 20 in (50 cm) high, known as the collared peccary, or in Trinidad as the quenk, a delightful name that I feel is particularly appropriate. Peccaries can be really fierce, and anyone meeting a mob of them is well advised to keep out of their way. They only have two enemies, the jaguar and humans, both of which consider them to be good eating.

Africa has its pigs as well, and giant forest hogs are huge, powerful animals that can be extremely irascible. It is funny how savage pigs can be, since they are highly intelligent animals and great personalities, though perhaps when you think that everyone in the world keeps trying to eat them it is hardly surprising that they have turned out the way they have.

Capybaras are not pigs at all but rodents. To look at they are like nothing quite so much as king-sized guinea pigs, which live in and around the rivers of south America, a continent which has its share of interesting rodents living in the jungles. Agoutis, acouchis and pacas all look much like rodents should look, though all of them are tail-less. They are all roughly the size of a cat, and spend their lives trying to keep out of everybody's way since they are regarded as suitable prey by any

> Indonesia has set aside 15 per cent of its forests for preservation. In the meantime the country earns US$1.4 billion a year from its timber, and most of the 300 major sawmills and 98 plywood factories were built after the government outlawed log exports in 1980.

Capybaras are huge rodents that live along the edges of rivers in South America. Harmless and shy, they are regarded as good to eat (*Adrian Warren*) ■

carnivore larger than themselves.

Some of the most interesting jungle carnivores must be the various birds of prey. There are plenty of the usual falcons, hawks, buzzards and so on, which is not to say they are not interesting, only that to the layperson they all appear much the same apart form their plumage, but when one gets to the eagles there are some extraordinary birds. One of my favourites is the harpy eagle from South America. It is a huge bird, and to my mind quite the most majestic of all the eagles. I used to keep one years ago, and I fell in love with her. On the other side of the world, in the Philippines, there is a rather similar bird known as the monkey-eating eagle. It looks rather like a manic harpy eagle on a bad morning with a hangover. Both these birds are very rare these days, and both of them feed on monkeys. In Cayenne, the capital of French Guiana, there is a small, horrible little zoo which displays a variety of local fauna. There are sloths and caiman and peccaries and harpy eagles, and the whole lot are fed on giant prawns since there is a prawn processing plant not far away at L'Arivot. It is quite ludicrous. If an animal will eat prawns it survives; if it doesn't it soon dies and is replaced with something else!

Rainforests are filled with such an enormous variety of life forms that it would be quite possible to write more than one book on that topic alone, and it is only possible here to sample an hors d'oeuvre composed of a representative selection. Some of the invertebrate life forms are spectacular, colourful and certainly should be mentioned, if only because they are often the ones most people come into contact with. Some of the most flamboyant animals of the rainforest are the beetles. If you think that beetles are small, black and boring, you should see some of the jungle species, for they are magnificent. Many are colossal, nearly as long as the page of this book, many have huge and fascinating horns, and lots of them are clad in the most beautiful colours to be found anywhere in the world.

In parts of the New World women catch some of the more attractive species of beetle, pull off the iridescent wing covers and thread them onto strings as necklaces. In Mexico there is a species of beetle known locally as the jewel beetle, which is a fairly close relative of the common mealworm beetle. These poor little animals are captured and pieces of coloured glass and beads are glued to their backs and a short length of chain is also glued to the animal, which is then pinned to the lapel of a lady's dress as a fashion accessory. There is an interesting story behind this custom. Apparently many years ago there was a handsome prince who was turned into a beetle by a witch when he was dressed in all his jewelled finery. His affianced princess was frightened that he might be trodden on before he could be changed back again into the man she knew and loved, so she fixed a small chain to the beetle prince and kept him pinned to her clothes while she searched for a suitable antidote or spell to change him back again.

An invertebrate I am fond of is the giant millipede. Though they are often disliked and even feared, they are harmless vegetarians, and various species can be found throughout the tropics. Centipedes, with which they are often confused, are a different matter altogether. They are often about the same size, 4–5 in (10–13 cm), but they are voracious carnivores which can run like crazy and are quite capable of injecting an excruciating dose of venom into a man. The daddy of all, is the giant centipede which can grow to the dimensions of a school ruler. They are huge and not to be messed with.

Is it not strange how some people like creepy crawlies like centipedes and others detest them, and one finds the same thing with birds and rodents and monkeys and all sorts of animals?

Until the 1960s there was a large international trade in the skins of various species of spotted cats for the fashion industry. Since then the numbers of animals have declined and popular feeling has made people far less willing today to be seen wearing a garment made from a spotted cat skin.

At one time the United States was the biggest importer of spotted cat skins, but that position is now held by West Germany.

One of the most exploited species was always the ocelot, found only in neotropical forests. As with other species, the numbers in trade have declined. Nevertheless, more skins are still traded than one might suppose.

Many ocelot skins were exported from Paraguay, but it has been illegal to export them from there for quite some time. It is thought that most of them had been brought illegally to Paraguay from Brazil, which also forbids their export.

Few rhinoceroses are forest animals. However, in the forests of Indonesia's Ujung Kulon National Park live about 50 Javan rhinos, one of the rarest animals in the world. Recent reports show that poachers have killed ten of the animals for their horns which are highly prized by Chinese pharmacists as a febrifuge and for a variety of illnesses. Contrary to Western belief, rhino horn is not used as an aphrodisiac.

Indonesia is also the home of the Sumatran rhino, whose population is down to 800. Horn from Indonesian rhinos is more highly regarded by pharmacists than that from African species. As a result the price is high enough to make it well worth the time and discomfort involved in hunting these Indonesian rhinos even in the dense jungle where they live.

Despite legislation forbidding the importation of rhino horn into places like Singapore and Thailand, it is not difficult to find the product in either of these countries.

THE CATS

Cats seem to be everyone's favourites and rainforests are rich in wild cats. Without any doubt the tiger is the biggest jungle cat. It ranges from India throughout much of Asia and is so well known that everyone must be familiar with it though until fairly recently much of its private life was still secret. Tigers are animals that keep to themselves most of the time and remain hidden in inaccessible places. For many years almost all one ever read of them was tales of man-eaters. Over the last century, due to the loss of habitat and the propensity of the empire-builders to shoot them, the poor tiger has had a difficult time. Its numbers declined to a very dodgy point. In India, after careful conservation by the government in conjunction with the World Wildlife Fund, the populations have crept up again, so that there are now more tigers in that country than there have been for quite a long period. Elsewhere this most magnificent of all cats is having a very lean time. Throughout its range, including India, it is protected, yet it is shot wherever it is found, and the skin is made into rugs and the bones are sold to Chinese pharmacists throughout the world who believe that they are efficacious in treating a variety of complaints.

The second-largest cat found in jungles is the South American jaguar. Many people get confused between panthers, leopards and jaguars. Panthers and leopards are the same thing. The former is the term most frequently used in India, while they are usually called leopards everywhere else in Asia, and in Africa. Some think that black panthers are a species on their own, but black leopards are just the same as the spotted ones except that they are a different colour. Jaguars are completely different. They are larger and bulkier, and are more aquatic in their habits, which is not surprising since, as we have seen, the jungles of the Amazon are as much water as land.

The other, smaller rainforest cats tend to get overlooked, which is a shame since they are beautiful little animals. They tend to resemble each other in appearance, looking for the most part like mini-leopards. Probably the only one that most people could name is the ocelot, but then they would probably only recognise it in the form of a coat. Funnily enough most pet-keepers who have a pussy cat tend to think that they feed on fish, but very few cats are fish-eaters. I am confident that most felines will take the odd fish if they are exceptionally hungry but it does not form part of their normal diet, though there is a fish-eating cat in South America, and a jaguar takes quite a bit of fish, together with rodents, deer and peccaries.

LIZARDS, SNAKES, AND CROCODILES

I wonder why it is that so many of us dislike snakes. Lizards do not evoke the same response, and plenty of people have kept tortoises and terrapins in their time. It is not even as though most snakes are dangerous since only about 10 per cent of the species in the world are venomous, and all of those would far rather leave you alone than bite you provided you do not bother them. (Once in India I slept for months on a pile of old nets in a room and only after quite some time did I discover that I shared my mattress with a cobra which used to come and go through a small drainage hole at the foot of one wall.) Despite the bad press they often receive, reptiles generally are no more repulsive than any other animal and many of them are exceedingly beautiful. So much so that in captivity one wonders how on earth they avoid falling prey to another predator. The fact is that in a jungle your chance of spotting any snake is very small indeed. Their camouflage is perfect. Despite that, some of them have evolved very sophisticated escape mechanisms. Most of the lizards can move very fast, and one lizard and one snake can actually fly, or to be more accurate they can glide, an excellent way of escaping an enemy. The lizard, which has the splendid scientific name *Draco volans* (flying dragon), extends

The giraffe stag beetle is found in the jungles of Malaysia. Although the formidable horns can give a painful nip, these animals are not in any way dangerous to man (*Peter Tryuk/ The Tropical Butterfly Garden*)

■

what appear to be wings on each side so that it can glide from one tree to the next, while the flying snake hollows its belly so that it glides on a long cushion of air. The snake's flight is not as controlled as that of the lizard, but it is still an effective means of escape.

Crocodiles are another group of animals that seem to be generally disliked, and appear to be regarded as ugly, yet baby crocodiles are lovely little animals, looking for all the world like freshly enamelled jewellery. I can understand someone refusing to accept that an adult crocodile is beautiful, but they are still majestic, powerful animals that one cannot help watching with awe, and with regard to their alleged ferocity one only has to watch the reluctant performers is a so-called crocodile wrestling show, in any one of the many tropical countries where such entertainments are provided, to realise that all the poor animals want is to be left alone.

Coral snakes from Central and South America are highly venomous, and brightly coloured in red, yellow and black. Many predators leave them alone. This false coral snake is harmless, but mimics the colouring of the venomous species in order to discourage predators (*Adrian Warren*)

■

All the animal life forms to be found in rainforests are highly specialised, beautiful examples of design, and many of them are only found in the jungles of the world. What is more, we may feel that we have learnt just about everything there is to know about the world we live in, but it is probably correct to say that every single zoological expedition to the rainforests of the world still finds completely new animals.

PLANTS OF THE RAINFOREST

TO WRITE A CHAPTER on the plants of the rainforest is rather like trying to write a chapter on the inhabitants of London or New York. The plants are every bit as varied as the people of those two cities. To most people the jungles of the world are simply tracts of wall-to-wall green, and we tend to forget how many of the plants that we take for granted came originally from the rainforest.

There is probably not a single home in the western world that does not contain timber that started life somewhere in a jungle, and although nowadays some tropical timbers are being farmed most are still taken from the wild. Mahogany, teak and many other ornamental hardwoods are rainforest species, and even broom handles and other objects that do not appear to be luxury goods come from the same environment. What seems surprising to me is that in the 'green' climate that exists today enough people still want such timbers to make it worth bringing them in. With a bit of luck before very long it will be considered as antisocial to buy a new mahogany coffee table as it is to smoke or to wear a fur coat.

Hardwood trees are perhaps the most obvious plants to come from the rainforest, and we have already talked of the rubber industry, but we also owe many of the things we eat to the jungle. Coffee and cocoa are both jungle plants though they are nowadays cultivated for the market. Peanuts too came from the same place, and just think of the number of different fruits that we eat that were originally from the forests. Fruits that in the West were only rarely seen until fairly recently can now be bought everywhere. In most markets or high streets one can buy mangoes and pawpaws, avocados and chicoos—from which tree, incidentally, we also get chicle, the raw material from which chewing gum is made—and lychees and star fruit. Another fruit,

There are many passion flowers in the forests of the New World, and many of them are flamboyant scarlet and crimson. This one is recognisable as a relative of the species commonly found in gardens (*Marion Morrison/South American Pictures*)

(OPPOSITE)
When the flowers of the cauliflory tree have been fertilised, it produces large fruit (similar to jackfruit) which are eaten appreciatively by man (*Heather Angel*)

The rambutan, a forest fruit closely related to the lychee, though the skin is covered in prickly hairs. When ripe the fruit are usually red (*Heather Angel*)

■

from the cashew tree, is the most thirst-quenching thing I know, and though it has not entered commerce yet, the cashew nuts can be bought in every supermarket in the country.

Even more exotic varieties of fruit like longans, jack fruit, custard apples and passion fruit are beginning to be more readily available, if not fresh, then in tins. One of the not-to-be-forgotten pleasures of a visit to the tropics is the fruit. Sadly by the time most of it arrives here it does not taste as good as it does when it is freshly picked, which is easy to understand since the fruit has to be picked while still unripe so that it can ripen when it gets here. In the meantime much of the natural sugar has turned to starch as the poor fruit struggles to stay alive. What always strikes me as odd, though, is that often the best varieties of some of these tropical fruits are not exported at all. In Britain I eat Venezuelan or Philippino mangoes as they come in season, and long for an Alphonso mango from south-western India. There is none to match it, yet I have never seen one outside that country. Come to think of it, perhaps the whole business does make sense. Alphonsos are appreciated by Indians as much as they are by me, and it would therefore be silly to send them abroad.

The most famous jungle fruit of all must surely be the banana. There can be few places in the world where it is not possible to buy a banana. They are now grown for the international market on enormous plantations in places like Central America and are shipped, still green, to our supermarkets. At one time that was all that happened to them but nowadays they are fumigated and treated with a disgusting combination of toxic chemicals in order to kill off any animal life forms that many be hiding among the fruit. Long gone are the days when it was possible to discover with delight a small, exquisitely jewelled baby snake hiding deep in the cool yellow hand of fruit, or a little tree frog looking up with wide, friendly eyes. It was not uncommon to find beetles or katydids in bananas either, and staff at banana ripening depots were used tc coming across spiders of all sorts, so much so that bird-eating spiders, or tarantulas as the Americans call them, came to be known as banana spiders in some places. Long ago I used to be called to the local banana ripening plant whenever such an animal was found. Contrary to what you might think the place was never in an uproar. The staff were certainly wary about handling the animals but they had become used to them and were never panic-stricken. They were always interested to know what an animal was, and whether it was dangerous. Only rarely did something like a spider get as far as a supermarket, but when it did the reaction was completely different. Much excitement ensued and the local newspaper reporter was sure to

Man uses a host of spices from the forest, including pepper, though nowadays it is grown on plantations such as this one in Sarawak (*Heather Angel*)

■

Logging within a rainforest is usually carried out by concessionaires who are only interested in a quick profit before they have to return their bit of forest to the government at the end of operations. Since the forest does not belong to them, the logging companies have no long-term interest in its future or in replanting.

A great deal of the destruction caused by

Although logging companies usually use giant machines to remove logs from the forest, sometimes they employ local labour to manhandle the timber to the road (*Andrew Frame/Survival International*)

■

logging operations is unnecessary. It has been discovered that if trees are cut so that they fall in a direction which will result in least harm, and then care is taken to remove them along the least damaging route, the

damage to the remaining forest is halved. Not only that, but the whole operation is less expensive and quicker. The huge, heavy machines used to extract timber today compact the soil to such an extent that seeds find it next to impossible to grow for a long while afterwards. The Skidders, the machines which are used to

remove the logs from the forest, tear great ruts through the ground, destroying the topsoil and the seeds and roots that it contains.

If the exposed soil that results from logging happens to be on a steep slope, a layer several centimetres thick can be lost in less than a year.

be called in to cover the story with much exciting detail. It always made a great story, but the animal was invariably harmless.

Rice made its appearance in the rainforests, and in places like Indonesia the plant is cultivated in paddy fields right to the edge of what is left of the jungle.

Brazil nuts are another item in our diets we take for granted that are found in the jungles of South America and, unlike many other foods, are still harvested in the wild. The seed pod falls to the floor and is collected by one of the many forest dwellers who supplement their income in this way.

FOOD AND DRUGS

The best way of learning about the plants within a jungle is from one of the people who live in the forest and make their living from it. The Amerindians are fantastic botanists and use many plants in one way or another. Many species of palm provide fruit that is eaten by humans, and the heart of a palm is also eaten by the forest people, though they will only do so if all other sources of food fail. They understand the need to conserve the resources of the world around them. It is sad therefore that western gourmets can buy tinned palm hearts from specialist delicatessens. The heart is the growing tip right at the top of the tree, and the tree must be cut down to remove it. The amount of food from a single palm heart is very small, and there is absolutely no excuse for them to be imported to countries like the UK. It is not even as though they taste very interesting. I have eaten palm hearts when I have had to in the wild, and really they are something no one would normally bother with, speaking from a culinary point of view. It is the mind-boggling waste behind it that gives them any appeal they might have for western gourmets, rather like the ancient Roman feasts of larks' tongues. The same sort of thinking goes into the demand for diamonds because we have to mine something like 10 tons of soil to obtain a single carat. If you could pick them up on the beach, things would be different (though at least diamonds are useful for things like drill tips). Maize is another useful plant that started in the jungles of the New World, and where would we be today without our cornflakes for breakfast? Potatoes come from the same source.

Our diets owe an enormous amount to rainforests, but perhaps nowadays the world of medicine benefits even more from their presence. Of the 30 million or so species of plants and animals on the earth, about two-thirds can only live in a tropical rainforest. Leaving aside every other argument for saving these incredible places, just think of the possible potential benefits waiting for humanity within their humid depths. As

Some traditional exporters of tropical hardwoods are now importing them. It is anticipated that The Philippines, Malaysia, The Ivory Coast, Nigeria and Thailand will all run out of timber for export within ten years.

When dried, gourds become very hard, and people throughout the world use them as containers (*Adrian Warren*)

(OPPOSITE)
Tree frogs are everywhere in the forests, particularly near water. After a heavy shower it is sometimes difficult to talk because of the noise of the local amphibian population (*Adrian Warren*)

During the course of each year about 20 million hectares of tropical forest are destroyed or degraded to such an extent that what is left is no longer viable. Some of the jungles are destroyed to provide the world with timber, and others are cleared so that the land can be used for other purposes such as farming cattle or growing bananas or other fruit. Often the forest is removed so that minerals can be extracted from the land. In some places the trees are burnt simply to provide charcoal to power the industrial plants in the area.

The fuel needs of local people also lead to forest destruction as wood is turned into charcoal for domestic purposes. The shortage of fuel wood in some places is acute.

Only very rarely do companies that plunder the rainforests replant any trees, and throughout the world less than 600,000 hectares of tropical timber plantations are established annually.

yet, less than 1 per cent of species have been looked at by scientists to evaluate their usefulness but already, apart from food and medicine, we have found resins and dyes, fibres and oils in the jungles of the world. What else might there be?

Quinine must be one of the best-known medicines that we use from the jungle. For a long time it was the only treatment for malaria. The Indians of South America first made use of it, chewing or making an infusion from the bark of the cinchona tree at the same time as they were using curare from another plant to tip their arrows so that when an animal was shot the poison would ensure it could not escape but would drop to the ground either dead or paralysed. When western doctors discovered curare it revolutionised anaesthesia, for tubocurarine is a valuable muscle relaxant.

One of the loveliest stories about a jungle plant and medicine must surely be that of the Madagascar periwinkle. This rather boring little plant with pink flowers used to live quite happily in the rainforest of the island of Madagascar. Then somebody decided to do a bit of experimenting with it, and while this process was continuing the habitat of the plant was destroyed and the plant disappeared completely in the wild. After a time the discovery was made that two chemical compounds from this periwinkle could be used in the treatment of leukaemia. Luckily the plant did well in captivity, and nowadays vast plantations of the stuff are grown to supply the pharmaceutical industry. As a result the survival rate of victims of leukaemia has risen from one in five to four in five. A nice postscript is that today one can also buy specimens of this plant from garden centres and nurseries under the name rosy periwinkle.

The contraceptive pill only became available so readily when it was discovered that the steroids needed to make it in commercial quantities were to be found in a Mexican yam.

With all the talk these days of drug abuse and the alarming spread of the cocaine derivative crack, it is easy to forget that cocaine is an invaluable drug that is used extensively in anaesthesia. When you visit your dentist he or she may squirt a dose of lignocaine or novocaine or one of its other compounds into your gums to prevent you feeling pain. Long before your dentist started to use it the ancient Peruvians had discovered its analgesic and narcotic qualities, and they regarded it as so important that to them the coca plant was sacred. To alleviate what nowadays seems to have been an often intolerable existence, the people of long ago Peru used to chew the leaves to help them get through each day.

The real scourge of the current times must be AIDS and after several false starts in the search for an effective treatment

The flowers and fruits of several forest trees grow directly on the trunk. This is a cauliflory tree, but the best known is the cacao tree (*Heather Angel*)

■

another drug from the rainforests, catanospermine, is now giving rise to real hope.

Some time ago the New York Botanical Garden undertook a study amongst the Indians of South America, and discovered that they make use of between 80 and 100 per cent of the plants around them. Thirty odd years ago the drug industry started to synthesise new chemical compounds as fast as it could, but today it recognises that even this astonishingly successful industry has its limits and that we need to go back to the forests, the largest gene bank this world possesses.

There are plenty of other useful plants in the rainforests of the world. Camphor comes from one of them, as does rattan, from which is made much of the furniture that fills the mail-order catalogues these days; and as we saw earlier many of our house plants started life here, and who knows what else there is that might be of use to us. But leaving aside the utility of it all, purely from a botanical and aesthetic point of view jungles are the most remarkable places. Relatives of the banana abound, ferns are everywhere, and there is nothing so pleasing as to walk quietly through a dark jungle and suddenly come across a flower of something like a spider lily, white, luminous and fragile, as seemingly out of place in that location as a set of false teeth on the pavement. Most jungle trees are evergreen, but some like the wild kapok are deciduous and may shed their leaves all at once before growing a new crop. The floor of the forest is the place to find ferns in profusion, especially along the banks of rivers: relatives of ginger, of the arum lily and of the ubiquitous African violet.

The chance of coming across Tarzan in the jungle is fairly remote though sometimes you feel he should appear at any moment since lianas are everywhere. They fix themselves to trees with small hooks or by tendrils as they reach ever upwards in the mad scramble for light. As with plants everywhere, these are especially adapted to life in their own environment and the more one looks at them the more one has to be impressed by details which a casual glance might not take in. For example, many rainforest plants have leaves with 'drip tips', long narrow tips on the end of each leaf to enable an excess of water to run off, thereby limiting the leaching of nutrients in solution.

Only in rainforests have I come across fruits that grow directly from the trunk of a tree, and this does seem to be a peculiarity of this environment. It has been suggested that the reason might be that some fruits are so huge that branches could not support their weight. I am not sure that I go along with this theory though it is true that some fruits are enormous. Durian and jackfruit are as big as footballs, and as heavy as the dreadful medicine balls that PE teachers used to torture their charges with

The British Ministry of Defence spends £650,000 a year on furniture made of afrormosia from the Ivory Coast, and £70,000 has been spent on rosewood veneer for officers' mess tables.

at school. Durians are especially savage since they are covered with viciously sharp bosses. One of those dropping on your head does not bear thinking about. Most westerners cannot abide the taste of durian fruit though it is loved by the people of the orient and by orang-utans. Someone once said that a durian tastes like heaven and smells like hell, and that is presumably why it is disliked outside the part of the world in which it is found. I love the stuff, and maybe the reason is that I have a nearly non-existent sense of smell. Cocoa fruit grow, like the durian, directly from the tree trunk. Until they have been pointed out it is almost impossible to see the very tiny white flowers sprouting from the bark which, when fertilised, turn into the cocoa fruit.

STRANGLERS AND CANNONBALLS

We looked earlier at bromeliads, and anyone travelling to south or central America or the West Indies cannot fail to notice them growing on trees and all sorts of unlikely places. They even grow on telegraph wires across the street. They are sold in nurseries as air plants, and have become very trendy in the last few years as ornaments for today's interior decorator, together with some species of *Ficus*, which are often known by botanists as strangling figs. They have slender stems or trunks and start life as epiphytic shrubs growing on the branch of a larger tree, using it as a support to reach the sunlight at the canopy. In time they put down aerial roots which eventually reach the ground. Where these branch and cross they often become grafted together and eventually a very strong basket-like structure encloses the trunk of the support tree. This continues to develop and it used to be thought that it could strangle the host tree and cause its death. This theory is now usually discounted, but it is quite possible for one of these strangling figs to outlive the host, and when that happens all that is left is the intricate hollow filigree of the strangler fig. Sometimes one comes across a host tree that has previously been surrounded by a strangler fig, but perhaps because the tree had a commercial or religious value for somebody the fig has been removed. When that happens one can often see that the trunk of the tree has been distorted or creased considerably where the strangler fig was.

In the apparently perfect growing conditions prevailing in a tropical rainforest one might be inclined to think that tree seeds germinate quickly and, where there is sufficient light, shoot upwards very fast, flower, develop seeds and die in a fairly short life span. Considerable research has been done on the subject and it has been shown that some trees are of considerable age. In Malaysia, studies into tree growth have resulted in figures of between 60 and 500 years while the oldest known tree in that

The Jari pulpwood project shows the extent of profitable schemes which result in the destruction of the Brazilian rainforest. On 1 February 1978 a floating power plant was towed out of the port of Kure in Japan. It arrived at its destination in the Amazon basin on 28 April, followed nine days later by a similar paper pulp mill. The plant weighed over 54,000 tonnes, cost US $269 million, and was designed to provide for the world's increasing demand for pulp wood. The power plant consumes 2,000 tonnes of wood a day which it converts into 55 megawatts of electricity.

Today the plant provides over 750 tonnes of pulp every 24 hours, worth about $500,000. In the mid-1980s the company stated that their aim was to clear 10,000 acres (4047 hectares) a year and replant them with fast growing commercial crop trees. The plant employs 30,000 people, and has its own airstrip, railway, and enough roads for its 700 vehicles.

The leaves of rainforest trees typically have drip tips to channel the water off the surface to the roots below. This ensures that the roots obtain the essential moisture, and prevents leaves rotting in the saturated atmosphere (*Adrian Warren*)
■

part of the world was a massive *Seraya* which was carbon-dated at 800 years.

I mentioned a durian crashing onto one's head, and the same danger lies in the rock-hard fruit of the Amazonian cannonball tree. One of the most frightening experiences of my life however was when I was sitting quietly at the base of a palm, waiting in the hope that the tapir I knew was in the area might come past, when a tremendous crash just behind me made me think that a tree had fallen. The noise was so loud and so close that I felt it must have missed me by millimetres, but finding that all my parts were still in working order I peered around the tree and could see no sign of a hole in the canopy nor a snow storm of fallen leaves glinting and flickering in a photogenic ray of sunlight that I could photograph. Instead all was as quiet and motionless as it had been. Then I realised that a single dead leaf had fallen from the palm beneath which I was sitting. The idea of a leaf hitting someone on the head might not seem very terrifying, but this single leaf was nearly 20 ft (6 m) long and so heavy that when I tried I could not lift it from the ground. On top of all that there were myriad sharp edges along the fronds, which would have ensured that, if I had been knocked unconscious, I would have been neatly sliced into chips as well.

Timber accounts for only 10 per cent of renewable resources when a rainforest is cleared, although many companies see the economic potential of a forest as being its trees. Instead of thinking in this fashion, companies ought to be aware that fruit, fibre, natural latex and medicinal plants can also be harvested, and that there is a far more viable economic argument for saving rainforests than those normally put forward by conservationists.

One of the most fascinating plants of the rainforest is not a tree but a water lily. The giant Victorian Amazon water lily has leaves that are many feet across. If you turn one over you can see that the underside is supported by a perfectly engineered system of veins and supports that are said to have inspired Joseph Paxton in his design for the framework of the huge Crystal Palace for the 1851 Great Exhibition of London. Some of these water lilies are grown at the Royal Botanic Gardens at Kew, and it is astonishing to think that they are grown anew each year and manage to put on so much growth in such a short time. There are photographs in existence of children sitting, lonely and frightened, in the middle of such leaves to demonstrate their size and strength.

On the jungle floor it is rare to see any plants in flower, either on the ground itself, or as far as one can see, though I have been fooled on occasion by spotting what I thought was a flower, only to find on closer inspection that it was a clump of brightly coloured butterflies. Funnily enough, wherever one goes throughout any tropical country one cares to mention, the locals will tell you that you should have been here three weeks earlier when the whole forest was a blaze of colour.

EXPLORING THE CANOPY

Few people are lucky enough to be able to look at the canopy of the forest from the canopy itself, but when you do get up there the view is breathtaking. It is no longer the featureless green that you have earlier flown over for mile after mile. The place is a wealth of colour. You would not believe there are so many greens in the world, though not all the leaves are green. Young leaves especially are often red or purple, and flowers and fruit can be seen after a little searching. It is extremely hard work climbing to the top of a forest tree, but well worth it when you get there, especially if one is able to move from the crown of one tree to another via walkways that have been erected previously. At first there do not seem to be many birds about but, as with any sort of animal, patience is required. One needs to develop the right sort of awareness, so that after a short while it can be observed that the canopy is packed with birds which are not as afraid of humans as are those nearer the ground, and consequently come far closer than anyone has a right to expect, and if you are in the right place hummingbirds will come over to investigate what you are wearing or carrying.

All this bird life, and insect life too for that matter, is in response to the fruit and the flowers that are everywhere. There is no other experience in the world to compare with a first exploration of a jungle canopy. To start with, the experience is terrifying as the tops of the trees sway alarmingly, and travel over

A brilliant heliconia flower brings a flash of colour to the generally sombre greens inside a forest. Heliconias are now being cultivated in Singapore for the cut-flower trade (*Tony Morrison/South American Pictures*)

(OPPOSITE)
Strangling figs like this one in Indonesia start life as seeds which germinate after being deposited on a branch of a tree. In time the plant grows, puts down aerial roots and eventually may completely hide the host tree (*Adrian Warren*)

■

the necessarily flimsy and flexible walkways is not for the faint-
hearted. I well remember waking one morning on a platform at
the top of a tree. I had tied myself in place the previous evening
with enough ropes to have kept the *QE II* in place in the event
of a hurricane. That day I did not wake slowly. I moved from
deep sleep to gibbering, terrified wakefulness in a single
moment.

FROM MONKEYS TO ANTS

From this viewpoint, watching primates and other mammals
rushing about teaches you all sorts of things that never occurred
to you before. On the ground or in a zoo, a monkey is a
monkey. In the canopy it is a cross between a helicopter, a
polybutathene ball and an Eddie Kydd. Watching a monkey
from below one can see only a silhouette and must always
assume that the animal will land where it is aiming, but from
above you become horribly aware of the amount of space
beneath. Yet if a monkey misses the branch it was aiming for
there does not seem to be any fear or panic. It simply keeps
falling, and as it does it keeps an eye out for any passing
branch. When it meets the right one it grabs it and continues
with what it was doing. One would imagine that after falling
the equivalent of a several-storey house before you catch a
branch, the least you would do would be to blow on your hands
to alleviate the pain, and wipe a hand across the brow, but
monkeys do not seem to see it that way. I have never known one
crash to the ground, though corpses with broken limbs have
been found on the forest floor, appearing to have fallen to their
death. Most monkeys either seem to have a death wish or to
possess a very devil-may-care attitude to life. I am sure this is not
really so, and that every move is calculated most carefully but
faster than any computer. Watch an orang-utan in the trees,
however, and you can see him working out where he is going to
put his hands and feet next. Big orangs are very heavy and
breaking branches must be a hazard to be borne constantly in
mind.

The canopy is an education in many ways. One of the first
things you realise is that the tops of all the trees do not
intermingle. The boundary of each tree stops a short distance
from the outermost leaves of the adjacent one. This
phenomenon is known as crown shyness and is thought to be a
defence against caterpillars. After all if they are munching holes
in your next-door neighbour, you want to keep your distance so
that they do not get you as well.

Remarkable little details like this are everywhere, and none
is more extraordinary than that of the leaf-cutter ants. As
everybody knows, every wildlife documentary proves yet again

The rainforest canopy is rarely seen by man. This part of the forest is rich in animals compared with the dark, silent floor far below (*Adrian Warren*)

■

Stalls selling live animals are a common sight in many Third World countries. Country people take the opportunity of capturing any specimens they can find during logging operations when hundreds of trees are felled within a short distance of their forest homes. On 10 August 1986 about 300 birds and mammals listed as protected species, and all from the country's rainforests, were confiscated from dealers in Bangkok, the capital of Thailand.

The deputy chief of the forest department, Phairote Suwannakorn, said that a team of officials led by Boonlert Angsirichinda had discovered a baby langur, a spotted jungle cat, a civet and several birds including a rare blue-winged pitta and a Siamese firebacked pheasant. All the traders escaped, having been tipped off in advance, leaving many thousands of bahts worth of stock behind.

Butterflies can frequently be encountered in swarms, often along the banks of rivers where they probe the mud with their tongues to extract essential nutrients (*Adrian Warren*)

(OPPOSITE)
One of the astonishing varieties of passion flower to be found in the jungles of South America (*Tony Morrison/South American Pictures*)
■

that there are constant streams of these little animals trudging along branches waving large pieces of leaf as they pass. They go to considerable trouble and travel long distances to get just the leaves they want, and do not think much of it if you get in their way. When they have each cut themselves a piece of leaf they carry it back to their nest which is deep underground. There the leaf is munched to a paste and this paste forms the base and food for a fungus that will be eaten by the baby ants. It is their entire diet and the amazing thing is that this particular fungus grows nowhere else on earth but in the nests of leaf-cutter ants.

Everyone who has spent any time in a rainforest will remember the ants. There are ants of many species everywhere

and the relationship of some species with plants is curious. The leaf-cutter ants use leaves to grow their fungus, while other ants actually live inside the hollowed-out stems and sometimes the thorns of some plants. There they live happily, protected from predators because of either the poisonous nature of the plant or because of its thorns. They return the favour by streaming out and attacking any invertebrate that strays onto their twig. The unfortunate intruder is bitten by as many ants as can get a hold with their jaws and it soon dies, thus ensuring that no plant-eating species of insect attacks the host plant.

The world of the plants is every bit as complex and fascinating as that of the animals that live amongst them.

90 acres (40 hectares) of tropical rainforest are destroyed every minute throughout the year. In about the time it takes to read this item we will have lost 50 acres (20 hectares) of jungle.

THE PEOPLE OF THE RAINFOREST

This Waorani hunter in Ecuador searches the treetops for a monkey to take back to his village for the pot (*Adrian Warren*)

■

The Jari pulpwood project in Brazil consists of a Japanese power plant and pulp mill. It cost US$269 million and consumes 2,000 tonnes of wood a day to produce 55 megawatts of electricity.

T IS A COMMON misconception that the human inhabitants of rainforests are few in number. In reality there are two hundred million tribal people in the world, of which the most part are rainforest dwellers. On top of this, one has to take into account the enormous numbers of humans whose families have moved to the forests even though their ancestors did not come from there in the first place. There must be at least as many of those as there are of the first group. Finally there are the people who live around the edges of rainforests and rely on them for at least a part of their livelihood.

Even though so many people in the modern world live in or around rainforests, this is only a tiny number compared with a couple of centuries ago. Throughout history the forests have been populated by the forebears of these people all of whom lived their traditional lives, no doubt as happily as any of us. It was only when outsiders began to explore and subsequently exploit the forests that they found themselves in trouble, which started right at the beginning of the invasion.

The forest people understandably took offence at strangers arriving to shoot and frighten the animals, to chop down trees that had helped sustain life for generations, and generally bring all the advantages of 'civilisation' to their previous lives. It must only have taken one Indian to shoot one interloper or vice versa for the whole business to snowball. The forest inhabitants had no chance against the rifles and shotguns of the outsiders, nor against the bacteria and viruses they brought with them, and before long their numbers were starting to decline. In many parts of the world which saw this sort of conflict, the Indians were regarded as yet another species of forest denizen to be regarded as sport, on an equal footing with monkeys and big cats. In some places bounties were put on their heads, and if

Dani tribesmen from Irian Jaya, Indonesia, in formal dress. The number of shells that form the bib of the man on the right represent his considerable wealth.

(OPPOSITE)
Dani tribesmen take a break from one of their ceremonies during the hottest part of the day (*Adrian Arbib*)
■

that sounds shocking and unlikely this sort of thing was continuing until very recently. Today most governments are willing to regard their tribal peoples as citizens with rights like anybody else, though one cannot help feeling that this is often only because of foreign opinion. But even with this new attitude towards them, forest inhabitants are often regarded as very much of a nuisance. There is a lot of money to be made out of rainforests, and anyone who is silly enough to want to live in the path of a bulldozer is regarded as an obstructive fool.

Many government officials in certain countries have expressed an opinion that such primitive remnants of a remote past must inevitably disappear in the name of progress. One of the troubles is that such people are regarded as ignorant and backward when in fact they are neither. They do well living in an environment that people from the developed world regard as impossibly hostile even with a wealth of modern aids to assist them. Forest dwellers are brilliant naturalists; their knowledge and ability to make use of the plants and animals around them is unsurpassed and impressive. Yet today there are less than 6

per cent of the original Indians living in the rainforests of the Amazon, compared with just before the arrival of the interlopers from outside. It says much for the good humour and patience of forest dwellers that they do not shoot every invader on sight, and I have always found them the nicest of people though they are often hard to get to know in the first place.

Nowadays it is probably the Yanomami Indians of Brazil and Venezuela that are attracting the most attention since it is their forests that are disappearing faster than any others. The first that many heard of them was when the World Wildlife Fund (as it was then known) commissioned an oratorio to be written and performed by a group of English schoolchildren. The piece was called *Yanomamo* and drew attention to the plight of the Indians. It is a moving, powerful piece that since its first performance has been toured throughout Britain and taken to America where it was greeted with as much enthusiasm as it was here. As publicity surrounding them grew, the Yanomamo proved to be remarkably well able to learn the skills of PR including the use of video technology.

Hummingbirds are only found in the New World, and though they occur from Argentina to the United States, by far the greatest number, 163 species, live in the rainforests.

The Yanomami Indians live in the dense forest of the Guyana shield in Brazil and Venezuela. Their culture and way of life have developed over many centuries and work very well for them.

Many Indians throughout South America have been very badly treated by the encroaching white men, often being regarded as game or pests and shot for sport or to clear the area. Even today many live in desperately miserable conditions on mean reserves. Wherever they are found, they are almost invariably at the bottom of the social heap.

The Yanomami are now threatened by the arrival of one of Brazil's new roads, the Perimetral Norte, which will cut through their previously impenetrable forest homeland. The rest of the world is now concerned about the plight of the Yanomami, but the Brazilian government shows little interest in their plight, even though appropriate noises are made in public about protecting them.

The Yanomami is now the largest remaining group of South American Indians, though there are still tiny remnants of other cultures in that part of the world. I have stayed with the Wai Wai for a while, and with the Oyampi on the borders of French Guiana and Brazil. Given the chance, they are happy to be left alone to live the life they have always lived, but in any small village or town throughout that area one can see Indians who have abandoned their traditional way of life in order to benefit from the advantages of developed society. They almost invariably have an awful job scratching a living at subsistence level by doing the most menial work. Again throughout the region one cannot help but be aware of the part Indian features in large numbers of Creoles that form the major part of the population in this part of the world.

CANNIBALS AND PYGMIES

On the other side of the world the jungles of Indonesia and Papua New Guinea belong to different countries, but the plants and the animals do not know that and as a result they look the same whether one is standing on the western side of the line separating Indonesian Irian Jaya from the eastern Papua New Guinea. It is one of the most exciting environments and is the home of the legendary birds of paradise. The island of Papua New Guinea is one of the largest in the world. While I was writing that sentence I began to wonder when an island ceases to be an island and becomes instead something like a continent. There did not seem to be a simple answer until my daughter came up with a perfect solution. 'Write', she told me, 'that any island smaller than Papua New Guinea is an island, and anything larger is not!'

On this island live some of the most remote peoples in the world who until recently had never come into contact with the last twenty centuries. The forest and the inhospitable territory meant that many villages were entirely isolated, cut off from each other completely, and as a result nearly a quarter of all known languages are to be found in Papua New Guinea. It is also the only place to find the rarest disease in the world, kuru syndrome, a dreadful condition in which fits lead ultimately to death. The disease can only be contracted by eating the brains of another human being—until recently the people of this part of the world were cannibals. One tribe, the Tasaday, were only discovered by westerners in 1971, and until the 1960s—when they discovered sago—they had lived entirely by foraging for edible plants and animals. There are only two dozen of these primitive people, living in the Philippines much as they must have done since the Stone Age.

In west Africa can still be found large tracts of rainforest

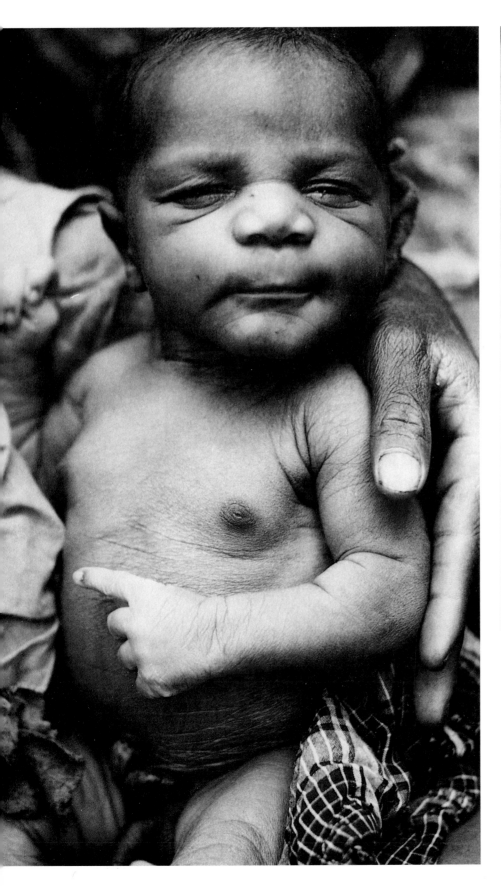

The pygmies of west Africa grow to a
height of about 4 ft (122 cm). Their lack
of stature and peaceful disposition
have placed them at the mercy of
other races, and at one time they
resorted to living in inaccessible caves
half way up a cliff face (*Survival
International*)

Pygmy babies have to be looked after
carefully by their mothers who do not
have access to modern medicines
(*Survival International*)
■

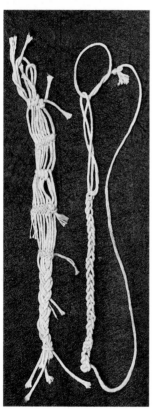

The pygmies of west Africa amuse themselves by making 'cats cradles' from lengths of cord (*Survival International*)

(OPPOSITE)
The Amerindian equivalent of 'bringing home the bacon'. This successful hunter is greeted with delight by the first person in the community to spot him (*Adrian Warren*)

■

within which live 150,000 pygmies. Some of them, the Mbuti from the Ituri Forest in Zaire, are probably the smallest people in the world, the tallest measuring only 150 cm (5 ft) in height. Pygmies are regarded by other west African forest dwellers as being the specialists when it comes to rainforest knowledge. They are regarded as having special skills and a kind of religious affinity with the gods and demons of the jungle.

The pygmies are great hunters and nobody climbs a tree as well as they can, though on one occassion in Trinidad I was astonished when the brother of the director of the Emperor Valley Zoo in Port of Spain suddenly slipped off his shoes and skittered up a tree in a few moments to grab a lizard belonging to the same family as the iguanas and which we had been discussing a moment before. Somehow one does not expect to see someone in a smart shirt and trousers, suitable for his day's work in the office, shin up a tree as efficiently as a pygmy. Some of the tribes of pygmies appear to be completely at home in the tree tops and wander about the branches with total equanimity. There is probably no animal in their forests that the pygmies will not eat, and they also consume ripe fruit with relish, though the one thing they love above all else is honey and they eat it happily whenever they can. The collection of honey from the nests of wild bees is not for the faint-hearted even though smoke is used to quieten the bees. The whole operation is more hazardous than it might be since the honey collectors wear no clothes at all. They seem to consider the risks acceptable and the whole group which accompanies a honey expedition happily munch away at pieces of honeycomb, wax, larvae and all.

HUNTERS AND HUNTED

Though the pygmies of west Africa are perfectly happy to climb trees, forest dwellers in many parts of the world are reluctant to do so and must use other means to obtain monkeys and other animals to eat from the branches above them. The two most common ways of doing this are using bows and arrows, and using blowpipes. Contrary to popular image, those that use bows and arrows when hunting do not fire into the trees at every monkey they see. They are remarkably reluctant to lose an arrow and this attitude is not difficult to understand. A good arrow is a time-consuming thing to make and there can be little more aggravating than to shoot it into a branch a hundred foot above one's head and watch a monkey wander away unharmed. I have never carried a gun in the tropics—I have never had any need to—and forest dwellers I have been with on various occasions have always become decidedly tetchy about this. They expect white men to carry guns and they would far rather have him shoot their prey for them than use their arrows unnecessarily.

Arrow poison frogs are tiny, brightly coloured amphibians that inhabit the rainforests of Latin America. The Indians of the Choco region of Colombia still extract poison from them even today, though in most parts the practice has died out as shotguns are commonly used rather than bows and arrows or blow pipes.

The toxins are extracted in an extremely cruel fashion, except in the case of a single species, *Phyllobates terribilis*. In this species the toxin is so virulent that a hunter has only to apply the tips of his arrows to the back of the animal.

The poisons are complicated chemical compounds. More than 200 different dendrobatid alkaloids have been identified. The most potent come from frogs of the genus *Phyllobates*. The poisons act on the nerve and muscle cell

The beautiful arrow-poison frogs are so named from the venom secreted beneath the skin. The liquid is extracted by some Indians and used to tip arrows and blowpipe darts (*Adrian Warren*)

■

membranes, allowing sodium to rush into them. This causes irreversible electrical depolarisation, which in turn results in sustained transmission of impulses and in due course death. Other toxins affect nerve impulses by blocking movements of vital ions.

The arrows are far longer than I ever expected them to be and are usually tipped with poison. When you think about it, it would be senseless going hunting without poisoned arrows because one rarely gets a clear shot at an animal since it is usually more than half hidden by branches and leaves. Consequently an arrow hitting it is not likely to do more than wound the beast which can then make its getaway. It might die later, but that is of no use to the hunter who shoots it.

The poison used to tip arrows is generally made either with a boiled concoction of plant juices which generally work as a muscle relaxant, or the poison from another animal, though I have only seen the latter being used in south America. There must be plenty of animal venoms which could be used but then you have the problem that when you come to eat the meat afterwards you might poison yourself as well. The animal poison used in Central and South America is obtained from amphibians, usually from one or another species of arrow-poison frog. The poor amphibian is spitted live on a long wooden skewer and slowly roasted over a fire. Venom oozes from pores in the skin and this is scraped off and collected. When enough has been obtained it is mixed with other ingredients and cooked into a paste with which the tip of the arrow is smeared.

I had always assumed that after being shot with a poisoned arrow an animal dropped to the ground within seconds. I

Waorani Indian cleaning the bore of his blowpipe. Unless the weapon can operate at maximum efficiency the hunter may not be able to eat (*Adrian Warren*)

discovered that this rarely happens and it can be literally hours before the victim succumbs. In the meantime the wretched beast sits on its branch clearly suffering until it finally falls. The hunter meanwhile waits patiently beneath, peering into the branches constantly and anxiously in case his supper recovers and walks away. When you stop to think about it this delay in the poison taking effect is not surprising since animals of all sorts have always reacted differently to the effects of toxins. Even in human anaesthetics different patients require different doses.

Hunters that use blowpipes are amazingly accurate. The pipe is not, as you might imagine, a simple tube. Much care is taken with its manufacture, and an inner, hollow stem is wrapped in an outer protective layer. The 2 m (6½ ft) or so length of the weapon has then to be tested and it is invariably the case that they do not shoot absolutely straight. Much experimenting needs to be done while the owner learns to compensate for any inaccuracies in his weapon. When everything has been discovered about its idiosyncrasies, sights made from animal teeth are set into it so that it will always be used to maximum efficiency. The darts that are used as ammunition are fairly long as well, and like the arrows they too are often tipped with poison. Blowpipe hunters, though, like the archers, are reluctant to lose darts if they can help it. I have practised with these remarkable weapons and have discovered with surprise that a comparatively small puff

A group of Penan children with a young gibbon. Dayaks frequently take any young animals that they catch to the towns in the hope of selling them for a little money. The survival rate of such animals is very low (*Sahabat Alam/Survival International*)

■

of breath results in a dart sticking into a tree trunk a considerable distance away. I have watched hunters use these things to shoot a tiny hummingbird from a distance at which I could hardly see it. When the hunters are shooting animals which they do not want to kill, they will tip their darts with small balls of hard latex which stun the prey. Hunters can earn themselves some additional income by collecting birds and other animals to sell as pets or to dealers for ultimate export.

Sometimes hunters use other methods of catching prey, and noosing seems to be practised by many cultures. The nooses are generally made from vegetable fibres, though perhaps strips of animal skin may be used sometimes. On one occasion I watched very small birds being caught with spider's web which is far stronger than you might think. And many forest people use a sticky substance, which we would generally call birdlime, to trap birds and other small animals.

In the forests of Borneo there is a tribe of nomadic, gentle

In the Malaysian state of Sarawak on the island of Borneo live a group of Dayaks known as the Penan. As is happening all over the world where people live in forests, their homes are disappearing in front of the giant logging machines.

The Penan, however, unlike many other people in this situation, refused to take it lying down, and in 1987 the loggers in the camps between Tutoh and Limbang had to be very careful indeed. The Penan had dug in their heels and refused to let any logging take place. The loggers could see no sign of the Penan but they knew that behind every tree there lurked men with blowpipes.

Some members of the Penan tribe of Sarawak. They defied the advance of loggers who were about to destroy their home forests. The government of Malaysia then prevented entry to journalists and other foreigners by ringing the area with troops. The current situation is unknown (*Andrew Frame/Survival International*)

All the roads had been blocked and work was at a standstill.

The Malaysian government has imposed a blackout on news from the area and no one knows what is happening at the moment. But any action by Malaysia against the Penan is going to have to be taken in the face of world disapproval.

people known as the Penan, who have become well known in recent years because of their objections to their forest being destroyed in the name of profit. Many nasty things were done to them a few years ago because they stood in the way of the developers. Luckily their plight hit the international headlines, so, although nothing was resolved and their future remains precarious, at least it is rather more difficult for anyone to practise genocide on them while the rest of us are watching. Not impossible, but difficult. All sorts of nasty schemes have been tried to get rid of inconvenient forest people. In the Mato Grosso of Brazil smallpox, influenza and tuberculosis were deliberately introduced into the Indians—not a century ago but in the early 1960s.

Somehow we are not as surprised as we should be when we hear of this sort of thing happening in Brazil or Borneo, but it seems far more shocking for some reason when it happens in somewhere like Australia. Little forest is left in this huge country, and what there is is along the northern edge. The government and local sources of money have decided to tear this last remnant to pieces as well, and when a year or two ago a determined group of protesters camped in the way of bulldozers they were removed with insensitivity, cruelty and disregard for the consequences, by police with dogs. One can understand the thinking behind a poor, Third World country trying to pay off crippling foreign debts by ruining its rainforests, but there is no excuse in somewhere like Australia, and in this case the individual police officers and the bureaucrats who sent them in, not to mention the contractors that asked for their help in the first place, should be thoroughly ashamed of themselves. To be honest I thought that many of the protesters were somewhat insensitive themselves. They knew there was going to be a violent confrontation and they still took small children and babies with them, which was an indefensible thing to do, but that does nothing to lessen the guilt of the forces of law.

EFFECTS OF WESTERN TECHNOLOGY

Hitherto we have been speaking of the indigenous inhabitants of the rainforests, but it should be remembered that plenty of other people live in and depend on them for their way of living. Any large tract of rainforest is sure to house communities of these other peoples. In Amazonia there are villages that started a century or more ago when escaped slaves met together and set up their new homes. In time these have expanded, very often resulting in the original inhabitants breeding with newcomers of other races, resulting in an interesting mix of types. Many of these communities do not take too much from the forest, though most of them own guns with which the men shoot a variety of animals to supplement the family diet. The greater part of the income for these communities comes from some sort of trade. There are still tiny, very scruffy villages where the men pan for gold or precious stones in the beds of the water courses and, just as they did long ago, many of them still exist on a diet that consists mainly of pig's tail, which accounts for their old name of pork knockers. Only rarely does one of these prospectors find a nugget or a stone that is worth very much, but they do seem to scratch a very precarious living, hoping desperately that tomorrow will be the big day when they will find the emerald that they know is just waiting for them.

Other small communities, often not more than one or two houses, manage to earn enough by hunting to stay alive. Even today when ocelots and other animals that have traditionally been collected for the fur trade are protected, one still finds hunters who make a steady but modest living by killing the animals and selling the furs to a dealer. Often the animals are

Probably no parrot in the world has been subjected to such an intensive management programme as the Puerto Rican parrot. This bird can be found only in an area of 4000 acres (1600 hectares) of the Luquillo Forest on the island that gives it its name. In the days when the island was covered in forest, it could be found everywhere. At present, it occurs only in 0.2 per cent of its former range.

In 1950 there were 200 birds on the island. By 1968 there were only 24 left, due almost entirely to the fact that suitable nesting trees had been destroyed. The dearth of suitable nesting sites led to battles and in 1974 two birds were killed as a result.

Artificial nesting sites were provided but at first the birds ignored them, and it was only after constant observation of their behaviour that sufficient knowledge was gained to provide nests that they would accept. The Puerto Rican parrot is still tottering on the edge of extinction.

Originally all the world's rubber was supplied from trees in South America. Although some is still produced in the region, the trade is now centred in the Far East, especially in Indonesia and Malaysia. Brazil used to be jealous of its rubber trade, as the demand during the Victorian era reached undreamt-of proportions.

At the time, one Clement Markham in the India Office in London saw that the demand was bound to increase, and felt that it would be of benefit to Britain to produce rubber in India rather than import it from Brazil. He approached a botanist named Henry Alexander Wickham, who was then living at Santarem on the Amazon, and

asked him to get hold of 70,000 seeds of the rubber tree, and bring them to England. Wickham managed to do this in 1876, with considerable difficulty and by means of much subterfuge, and the seeds were germinated at Kew Gardens.

At first the small rubber trees were planted in Ceylon (Sri Lanka) where they failed miserably, but in

Even though the rubber industry is now concentrated in south-east Asia, some rubber tappers still eke a living in Brazil. As the forest disappears, so does their way of life (*Adrian Warren*)

∎

time plantations of them were established in Malaya, and half a century later the face of the rubber-producing industry had changed for ever.

trapped rather than shot, and beaten or strangled to death in order to prevent a hole in the skin and to save the cost of a cartridge—a small sum to you or me, but a considerable outlay for a poor hunter.

Some communities concentrate on collecting live animals which eventually go to exporters in the major towns. Their stock in trade may be monkeys or birds or lizards—all sorts of things. In many cases this sort of collecting does no harm to the wild populations though occasionally it has done. Squirrel monkeys in South America have been shipped out for medical research in such huge quantities over the last half-century that they are decidedly thin on the ground, or at any rate in the trees, in

Dugout canoes are commonly used as transport, even today. Making them is laborious work. When a tree has been cut and hollowed-out to make a canoe, stretchers are placed across to prevent warping. Afterwards, a fire is lit beneath and inside the canoe to harden and seal the wood. When the canoe has cooled completely the stretchers can be removed (*Adrian Warren*)

places where previously they were common.

I asked a friend in India where all the monkeys I remembered from my childhood in that country had disappeared to. They are all in your country now, he told me, adding after a pause, and in America.

It is a lovely idea to imagine that the people of the rainforest would like to remain noble savages for ever and, whereas plenty do not want to see any change, it is only fair to point out that many cannot wait to incorporate western technology into their lives. After all, when a river journey which takes ten days with a paddle can be reduced to four or five hours while you contentedly steer a canoe with an outboard motor on

WHY ARE RAINFORESTS IN DANGER?

RAINFORESTS HAVE TAKEN MILLIONS of years to turn into the complex environments they are today. Throughout the history of humanity, human beings have been living in and around those forests, killing the animals that live in them, cutting down trees, and removing parts of plants to eat, all without doing the forest any harm at all. Then, after World War II, there were a whole new batch of technological development that enabled us to travel to the moon, cure disease that had been killing us for centuries, get from A to B at a speed of a mile a minute, and use machines to cut and dig at a hitherto unimagined speed.

We were now able to take a rainforest to pieces at an unprecedented pace. If anybody asked why we should do this, no one answered that it would benefit mankind because we might discover new medicines, or thereby learn to feed the previously starving peoples of the world, or find out how to produce non-polluting sources of fuel for our vehicles. The decisions were taken on purely economic grounds. Get rid of the rainforests and we can increase our profits. Since, luckily, not everybody is the same, along the way some invaluable finds were made, but I do not believe that any decision to destroy rainforest was taken for any other reason than to increase shareholders' dividends.

Once the technology had been developed all sorts of possibilities occurred to the boards of the big multinational

Once the valuable big trees have been removed, small plants are destroyed by burning. Afterwards local people try to grow crops on the open spaces but they do not do well on the poor soil, which in any case is soon washed away by the next rains (*David Potter*)

(OPPOSITE)
The slash-and-burn culture of many forest people has been practised for centuries and done no harm. Here a hut is burned prior to moving to a new area. Modern wholesale clearing and burning for profit destroys forests forever (*Adrian Warren*)

∎

Roads are being made through rainforests everywhere. To prevent the banks collapsing onto the road at the next rains, they have been terraced. This technique is only marginally effective (*David Potter*)
■

In the developed world we use 200 million tonnes of wood each year simply to make paper, and as the level of literacy grows, the demand increases. Third World countries use 25 million tonnes. The amount used by Brazil doubled during the 1960s and again in the 1970s, and in five or six years time it will have increased by half as much again.

Many Third World countries cannot afford to import wood pulp in these quantities; indeed some of them spend as much doing so as they earn exporting hardwood. The result is that more and more of them are now producing their own wood pulp.

Of all the wood used in the world, only 37 per cent is softwood. Pulpwood and paper account for a further 29 per cent, plywood and other laminated boards use up 13 per cent and hardwoods make up the final 21 per cent.

companies. Just look at the advantages to ourselves, they said. Not only can we immediately increase our profits, but we can raise everybody's standard of living as well. What they actually meant was that with all these potential sources of revenue available to them in the forest, they could create new markets around the world until these products were regarded as invaluable, and sales would increase beyond all their hopes.

LARGE-SCALE CLEARANCE

So one day somebody went out to a bank and borrowed some money to finance the first of these projects, and with the money he went and bought mechanical diggers and cutters and ships and men, and sent them all off to the remote parts of the world where rainforests grew. No one in those days gave a thought to the ultimate effects of such vandalism and indeed we did not have the scientific knowledge to understand what would happen. The first and most obvious advantage to our company was the timber that was found. No longer did it take days or weeks or months to locate a single valuable tree and to cut it down and get it back to civilisation with an enormous amount of labour of men and elephants. Valuable timber trees do not generally grow in useful-sized clumps in the forest. They grow singly, so, having found one, it might be quite a while before you found the next one. Now it was possible to clear great swathes of forest in no time and reveal valuable trees emerging all over the place. The business was terribly wasteful as for each tree with a commercial value that was removed, enormous numbers of other plants were destroyed as well.

Roads had to be built to enable vehicles to get deep into the jungle, encampments had to be cleared of undergrowth and, as each tree was felled, it was dragged by vehicle to the nearest road, tearing great holes in the jungle behind it. This does not take into account the fact that, for each cubic foot of timber obtained, at least as much was left behind in the form of small branches, leaves and so on. Local people were horrified to see what was happening, but, ever ready to make the best of their surroundings, they burnt off all the now dead scrub and found that they had at their disposal, for the first time, what appeared to be limitless fields in which they could grow crops. It must also have seemed that the soil would be very fertile since an enormous great jungle was growing on it. However, as we have seen, the soil of a rainforest is a rotten place to plant a crop. Nutrients were soon used up, winds blew away any topsoil there might have been, and the first rainy season after the forest had been burned washed nutrients, soil and newly planted crops down the nearest river. However, that was of little interest to the board of directors on the twenty-fifth floor.

They were delighted with the pound notes that were filling their bank vaults as a result of this timber. But no business stands still, and it did seem a shame to waste all that bare red soil. The only other place to look for more money was under it, and once the first surveyors started to dig they found that beneath the soil of places like Amazonia there were minerals in undreamt-of quantitites. Telexes were sent, more money was raised from banks, more equipment was dispatched and great holes started to appear in the ground as bauxite, iron and 101 other commodities were hauled from the earth.

While all this was happening, people in other businesses watched idly at first and then wondered how they could get their hands on a share of the profits. It was not long therefore before other types of business began to move in, nor were any obstacles put in their way by the governments concerned. After all, when someone comes to you and offers you several million pounds for the rights to dig a hole in what appears to you to be a completely useless part of your country, you would be an idiot to refuse, especially as in the meantime you have taken on very

The typical red soil of rainforests. This road was built by the French Foreign Legion to open up the interior of French Guiane, but the project ran out of money, and round this corner the road stops dead (*David Potter*)
■

large loans from banks around the world to keep up your own tottering economy. Such opportunities must have seemed heaven-sent. Here was a chance to reduce the crippling interest payments, and perhaps make a profit at the same time. What is more, maybe one could also win some advantages over these big successful foreign countries at the same time. For years they had been colonising and exploiting countries like yours, and at last this was a chance to get back at them and increase your own precarious standing in the eyes of your electorate, for being the leader of a Third World country is no sinecure. There is a very real chance in many of them that you will not only lose your job, but your head as well. So everybody was happy, apart from the people who lived in and by the jungles, and what did they matter anyway?

The new companies that moved in did so primarily for two reasons. The first was to grow crops for the affluent West. Thousands upon thousands of banana trees were planted in what had previously been rainforest in Central America. Unlike for the poor peasants who lived there, the lack of nutrients in the soil did not matter because these large companies had plenty of cash to add nutrients by the ton which they imported from elsewhere. Soon bananas, sugar and other crops were leaving by the shipload and, for these companies too, the profits increased. And then came what was perhaps the most unlikely newcomer of all. For the first time in half a century or more the affluent parts of the world, having recovered from two world wars, had money to spend, and the era of the fast-food joint arrived. More or less from the beginning they were condemned by everyone as

A year before this photograph these hills were covered in rainforest. A year later, even the few remaining trees had disappeared. Throughout the world the same picture is repeated endlessly (*David Potter*)
■

providing food that was unhealthy and likely to lead to heart disease and all sorts of other avoidable conditions, but nevertheless these places were instantly popular with children and teenagers. Even today they are still expanding, and turn up in the most unlikely parts of the world where hamburger-and-chips takes over from what the locals have been eating for centuries.

It worked so well that the companies that supplied the food suddenly found that they could not keep up with the demand or, if they could, it was impossible to provide the products at one economic price. It takes a lot of space to grow cattle; one can grow a far higher weight of chips on an acre of land than of beef, and another disadvantage of the increased numbers of cattle was that they provided such mountainous quantities of dung, and in places where land is at a premium, what do you do with the stuff? Somebody had the great idea that here was mile after mile of cleared land in places like South America that was just asking to have cows trotting about on them, and this is what happened. The cattle barons moved in. Initially the land was still only capable of growing crops as poorly for them as it had for the peasants, but a by-product of cattle is all this

Erosion is destroying the forest on the hills on the right. When left to itself, as on the left of the picture, the forest maintains an equilibrium (*David Potter*) ∎

111

A few days previously the whole of this area was covered in forest. The rate at which the trees are being felled is beyond comprehension. This is Sarawak, part of Malaysia where the government has made it illegal to publicly criticise logging companies (*Andrew Frame/Survival International*)

(RIGHT)
An employee of a logging company makes the first moves towards felling a tree (*Marcus Colchester/Survival International*)

■

splendid dung that was now no longer a problem, but rather a
most valuable resource when spread upon the land. Soon crops
of grass were flourishing and scrawny cattle grazing happily upon
it while they waited to become hamburgers.

This was the situation for twenty years or so. Everyone was
happy raking in the profits and the banks were delighted to lend
ever greater sums of money to finance such ventures. True, there
were conservationists around the world who expressed their
concern but, damn it all, they were only cranks. And those that
were not were made to appear so by the companies that were
exploiting the rainforest so that the conservationists would not
be taken seriously, in case this caused someone to question these
methods of making money.

Then in the 1970s one or two people began to get alarmed

**One in five of all the
birds in the world live
in the forests of the
Amazon.**

In 1989 the Massachusetts Audubon Society formed an alliance with the Belize Audubon Society to try and save a huge area of vulnerable forest in the Central American country of Belize.

The idea came when Coca Cola donated 42,000 acres of rainforest as a reserve, following international criticism of its plans to develop forest land by replacing it with citrus plantations.

Surrounding this site is an area of 210,000 acres (85,000 hectares) of rainforest which the present scheme is designed to save. Anybody wishing to help can do so by sending a minimum of £25 to Programme For Belize, PO Box 99, Saxmundham, Suffolk, England IP17 2LB. This enables you to purchase a small area of the rainforest in perpetuity; in return for the money you receive a signed certificate of purchase.

The scheme is sponsored by Tate and Lyle. US$6.7 million is needed if it is to succeed. Already many companies and organisations are joining the host of individuals helping to save Belize's rainforests from further destruction.

Belize is a small, exquisitely beautiful country in Central America. Much of it is covered in rainforest, and as yet it is unspoilt. Known until fairly recently as British Honduras, it is now independent and under enormous pressure to be developed. Already large multinational companies are altering the nature of the country. However, the indigenous people, and there are only around 170,000 of them, are keen to protect what they can, and the country boasts several reserves.

In order to satisfy the apparently insatiable US demand for orange juice, one company has acquired 200 square kilometres of forest to plant orange trees, and has a stake in another 2400 square kilometres.

It remains to be seen whether Belize will become trapped in the destructive cycle of debt and development, as happens so often with newly independent countries. It is sad to see a recent article in *The Financial Times*, headed 'An Uncut Jewel Waiting to be Exploited'.

and to wonder what was happening. Populations of animals started to decline, and so did plants in some parts of the world, especially in previously rainforested areas. Timber began to increase in price as trees were used up, and tourists that used to visit countries to see all the things that the place was famous for began to ask what was happening to it all. Television documentaries started to be made which asked the same questions and many people felt concerned. All except for the companies who continued to earn all this lovely money. No problem, they said. These worries are all needless, they would tell us at press conferences, and then they would drive home to their teak-filled homes, picking up a parcel of hamburgers on the way for the family, before they disappeared into their mahogany-framed greenhouses to water their orchids.

CITES

It was time something was done. One of the first things that happened was that representatives of many countries around the world got together in Washington and came up with a document which has since come to be known as the Washington Convention on International Trade in Endangered Species of Plants and Animals. The document came to be known generally and simply as CITES, using the initials of the key words.

The signatories of CITES agreed that they would monitor

trade in plants and animals between their countries. Animals and plants were all listed and, depending on how common or otherwise a species was, it was placed on one list or another. List 1 for example contains all those species in which any trade at all is likely to affect the continued survival of the animal or plant. Trade in these species is banned except in exceptional circumstances. Each country then brought in its own legislation to make this work, and usually went further than that, so that plants and animals were protected along the same lines within every CITES country. The whole business, as you might imagine, was a lot more complicated than that, but by and large that was how it worked.

Since then more countries have joined, and today there are 101 members. Any country which expects anyone to take it seriously with regard to its attitude to the environment is a member of CITES. It soon became clear that several of the countries who had signed CITES really could not give a damn about the plants and animals of their country and had only signed to show the rest of the world how caring they were. They brought in legislation in their own countries but this legislation was for the most part not implemented, and illegal logging and trade in banned species continued as enthusiastically as ever, quite often with the connivance of government departments and their ministers and officials. Indeed many of them had shares and influence on the boards of the companies that were still trading in these now illegal commodities. At least one country continued to flout the whole spirit of CITES to such an extent that it was finally thrown out. Another country for years refused to join, saying that there was no need for it to do so since it supported all that CITES stood for, and in any case it had its own laws along much the same lines. All this while it was known around the world as one of the major abusers of wild plants and animals. Just recently it did join, but even so there is no problem at all finding banned products for sale. Within an hour in the place one can discover stocks of rhino horn, ivory, tiger skins, timber of all sorts, strictly protected specimens of various pitcher plants and a host of other goodies, all of which should not be there.

I was amused recently, by some news that reminded me of a bird dealer from this same country who is regarded as one of the top-ten baddies by customs forces around the world. He quite blantantly trades in all sorts of illegal species. However, public pressure and a ban by the USA on the importation of tropical fish from this place finally persuaded this country to join CITES. After a couple of prosecutions of this trader for continued illegal trading in parrots following its new status, the country fined him very small amounts of money that hardly cut into the profits on

Indonesian forests are being devoured to serve man's need for hardwood. Many of the trees are chopped into tiny pieces to make chipboard (*Adrian Warren*)

■

Many of the plants and plant products that we use were originally found in the rainforests. This is wild ginger from Papua New Guinea. Bananas, quinine and cocoa are other forest products in every day use around the world (*Brian Rogers/Biofotos*)

∎

the birds concerned. However the new situation was such that he clearly thought that the time was right for him to move the illegal part of his operation elsewhere, and this he did to a small country in Europe, paying a certain person in the government a very large sum of money on the understanding that this would enable him to continue trading without, as they say, let or hindrance. This was guaranteed and he breathed a sigh of relief. It was therefore with much amusement that I saw the other day that this same country has now joined CITES itself!

The trouble is that it is very difficult to persuade many countries that there is a need for conservation. At least in places like Britain, Europe and North America people have been brought up to enjoy plants and animals. After all, most households have either a garden or some house plants, and, even if they do not have at least one family pet, they do regard going to a zoo as an entertaining, interesting day out. On top of that we are constantly seeing programmes about something to do with the environment so that most people are aware of the problems even though they might not be interested enough to want to do anything more about them.

In other parts of the world the situation is not the same. In many places a plant or an animal is either regarded as a source of income or as something to eat, and if it does not fulfil either of these criteria it is of no significance, and it is no use trying to persuade such folk that conservation for a variety of other reasons is important. It is extraordinarily difficult to put across the other countries' attitude towards plants and animals to someone in the West who has not had experience of it, and the best way I can try is to relate the wild plants and animals in other countries to the way we think about empty crisp packets. They are all over the place in this country and for the most part we do not even notice them. If someone came to us and suggested that they were willing to pay 50p for each crisp packet that we collected and took to him, we would immediately find ourselves interested in them and we would notice them. Until then they are around and of no consequence, and that is how many people in the world feel about their native flora and fauna.

Since individuals think like this it is sometimes extraordinarily difficult to persuade governments to change their thinking as those governments are made up of individuals with the same attitude to the enviroment. It is especially difficult when, as we saw earlier, there are what seem to them to be good sound economic reasons for letting people exploit their rainforests. Some countries are concerned, and are trying with varying degrees of success to stop illegal logging and despoliation of their forests. Others are particularly intractable. At the moment Brazil refuses to listen to reasoned argument. It is

The only British company still logging in Sarawak says it only removes two trees per acre, but under questioning admits that this results in the destruction of 40 per cent of the forest.

The attractive flower of the Costa Rican gurania is from the same family as the infinitely better known cucumber (*Brian Rogers/Biofotos*)

∎

Indonesia is a collection of 13,677 islands in south east Asia, 992 of which are said to be permanently inhabited. It is an extraordinary and beautiful country that until fairly recently was well covered in forest. The island of Java, where the capital, Jakarta, is to be found, is the most densely populated island, with 95 million of the country's 150 million people. South-east Asia exports three-quarters of all the tropical hardwoods traded, and Indonesia's contribution equals more than that of all the other south-east Asian countries combined.

In 1970 280 million cubic feet (8 million cubic metres) of timber were taken, double the amount of the preceding year. Three years later the figure was more than double again, and today 10 per cent of Indonesia's income is derived from the export of timber.

By 1980 the rate at which Indonesia's forests were being destroyed was estimated at 1.5 million acres (600,000 hectares) a year, and a map of Sumatra or Kalimantan or Irian Jaya will show that logging concessions have almost reached saturation point.

difficult to make countries understand that they must not continue to destroy their forests, that they have no right to do this. It is just as difficult to persuade the present British government that it too has no right to continue to allow businesses to persist in emitting gases into the atmosphere that result in acid rain that ends up destroying trees in Europe. The reply that always seems the most spineless to me is that which claims there is no firm proof that . . . (you must have heard it). I feel very strongly that, if there is a possibility that any course of action might be harmful, that action must be banned until proof is obtained either way.

There are alternatives to everything, and conservation will only work when it is financially attractive. Only when the consumer refuses to use a product is a producer going to change it. In this case of globally important issues, governments must play their part in encouraging research into alternatives.

THE EFFECT OF FOREST CLEARANCE

When one visits a part of the world where rainforests have been removed it is easy to see the effect on local people, because, make no mistake, what we are talking about is people, not trees or animals. In addition the wider effect is often considerable, and until recently was almost always unforeseen.

Bangladesh is a case in point. It is a very flat country, much of it on or about sea level. To the north are the thickly forested Himalayas. Much of the timber has been removed from this lovely range of mountains with the result that whenever the monsoons come there are no forests to soak up the water, and no root systems to hold the soil together on the south-facing slopes. Whoosh, away it all rushes and before long Bangladesh is covered with water and people are dying. Their homes are destroyed, their livestock is killed and they themselves drown. Before long the stagnant water becomes full of rotting carcases and faeces with the result that it turns into a rich biological soup in which germs breed in their countless millions. In turn they infect the Bangladeshis who start to go down with typhoid, cholera and other serious conditions and, as if all this was not enough, the higher water levels mean that the holes which are inhabited by venomous snakes can no longer be regarded as desirable abodes by the reptiles, which are forced to emerge. When they make for any solid surface above the level of the water they find it already crowded to capacity with cold, miserable, wet human beings. In the circumstances it is not surprising that even more people die, bitten by snakes.

Recently I was in Thailand, a beautiful country that I love dearly, populated by super people of whom I am very fond. It has lost something like four-fifths of its rainforest in the last

Indonesia has been criticised internationally for the insensitive removal of many of its citizens from their homes to make the land available for logging or agriculture. These unfortunate Asmat tribespeople stand before their new home in a resettlement village (*Adrian Arbib*)

A cattleya orchid from Brazil. Cattleyas and other orchids are developed by the horticultural trade for their showy blooms (*Brian Rogers/Biofotos*) ■

thirty odd years. I was talking one day to a friend, Katy Buri, who had recently been for a couple of weeks to camp in the Khao Yai national park. It was some time since her previous visit and she was telling me how the place had changed. On this latest visit, she said, all her party came back black from the layer of ash that covered everything, and in all her time there the only bit of wildlife she saw was a single deer. Khao Yai is regarded as the most prestigious national park, yet hunting and illegal logging continue apace. There is not a reserve in the country where one cannot hear the sound of shooting, and it is not uncommon to see timber being removed within sight of notices forbidding it. I have watched patches of protected forest being burnt after the commercial timber has been removed, while reserve guards have stood by sharing a cigarette with the men lighting the fires and watching the flames reach up the remaining trees.

Each weekend there is a huge market just outside Bangkok, the capital of Thailand, where a customer can buy goods of all sorts from pottery to plastic spoons to traditional musical instruments to live parrots. Each week one can see species of animals and plants for sale that have come down from the forests in the previous few days, rescued by enterprising villagers to make a few coppers rather than let them die where they fell.

Thailand is not alone in this; it is happening all over the world and I have seen the same sort of thing in Malaysia and other places in the Far East, in Central and South America and in Africa. The sad thing is that one can read umpteen books about all this destruction, or watch picture after picture of it on television but these do not have anything like the same impact as a trudge across a range of hills, feet throwing up little puffs of ash as you walk through mile after mile of the stuff in a place which a couple of weeks previously had been rich, thriving, active rainforest.

A mistake commonly made is to assume that the local people make money out of all this, that they are employed by the loggers on a daily basis, and that they can salvage animals and plants from the destruction to sell. The real truth is that only one or two will be able to make themselves a few pennies in one of these ways. What actually happens is that the first many villagers know about it is the arrival of the first of the vehicles. The locals all gather by the road to watch with awe as these enormous machines roar and lurch into the forest. Within hours a preliminary camp has been erected and within days the first logs are being dragged from the forest and loaded onto the waiting lorries. A few weeks or a few months later the whole circus moves on. All the workmen and the vehicles are hired in the big towns, and all the profits go to the investors far from the

A drug obtained from a plant known as the Madagascar periwinkle, now extinct in the wild, has increased the chances of survival for children with leukemia from 20 to 80 per cent.

This Akha girl from northern Thailand is wearing a typical headdress which she will remove only occasionally throughout her life (*Elaine Briere/Survival International*)

∎

slopes where the timber is removed.

It is difficult to indicate the scale of such projects, for some of them involve much more than the use of a few hundred or even a few thousand trees. There is an opencast mine in Brazil that is some 20 miles across and, if that sounds like an enormous project, think about the Jari pulpwood project, which is mind-boggling in its scale. In the late 1970s a shipping magnate had a great idea. He calculated that a few years thence there would be a world need for pulpwood and he thought he should be the chap to satisfy it. Pulpwood is used for all sorts of things from newspaper production to the filler for those collapsed kitchen units you buy from a warehouse down the road and take home only to discover that three screws and one sheet of the instructions are missing. Daniel K. Ludwig, for that was the shipping magnate's name, had a dream of planting trees in rows on fields so huge that from the air they would look like fields of corn.

The original idea had been in his mind for some years before anything happened, while he thought about the technology involved and wondered about a possible site for his scheme. Eventually he raised the necessary cash and went to

Japan to have the plant built. It was not to be an ordinary plant, he told the designers. It must be entirely self-contained and built on a hull so that it could go on a sea journey until it arrived at the site where it was to be put to work. Where might that be, they asked, and were told that the whole business was to be in the middle of the Amazon rainforest at a place called Jari.

The production plant (and that is an ironic name if ever there was one) was made in two parts. One was a pump mill and the other was the power plant to drive it. Each of these units was built onto its own sea-going hull. Nothing of this nature had ever been made before so it was all a bit of a gamble, and on 1 February 1978 the power plant set off from Japan on its long journey right round the world to Brazil. It weighed 30,000 tonnes and was far too big to fit through the Panama Canal so it had to go the long way, south to the Philippines, west to southern Africa, round the Cape of Good Hope and then across the long haul of the south Atlantic until it arrived at the mouth of the River Amazon. It was pulled and pushed on its journey by a number of tugs, and considerable calculation and luck was needed to ensure that it met no bad

Transmigrants, forcibly removed from their homeland by the government, have considerable difficulty scratching a living from the poor soil of cleared forest (*Adrian Arbib*)

(OPPOSITE)
Extensive logging is taking place in the Asmat region of Irian Jaya, Indonesia. The logs are rafted down the rivers to the sawmills. The crews of the rafts live aboard them in flimsy huts (*Adrian Arbib*)

(OVERLEAF)
A Venezuelan river trails slowly through the jungle. The outside of each bend becomes more eroded where the flow is fastest, and material is deposited on the inside in the form of a beach. Eventually a loop can join up, forming a lake which can eventually be cut off from the river (*Adrian Warren*)

■

weather on the way. It took three months to arrive, and nine days after it set out from Japan its partner, the power plant which was to run the whole operation, also set off to follow in its wake.

One small boy who was fishing when the first of these monsters arrived quickly paddled back to his hut to tell his disbelieving parents that a city was coming up the river. The two plants were moved side by side into the place designated for them, and before long they were ready to start work. The first thing was to remove any commercially valuable trees from the area of jungle that was going to be used for producing the pulpwood. After that there was no further obstacle to clearing the jungle quickly and efficiently, and before long it was being burnt as far as could be managed. In the 5,600 square miles (9,000 km²) of black ash remaining after the burning, small fast-growing seedlings of pulpwood trees were planted. They were eucalypts, melina and various conifers. Before too long the enterprise was in production.

Today the statistics provided by the place are remarkable. More than 30,000 people are employed by the plant, most of them locals, so a whole town has been born to house all these

Many of the small rainforest plants can be overlooked even though there are multitudes of them. Mosses and algae cover the branches of many trees, and fungi are everywhere.

Once an area of rainforest has been logged, even if it is given the rare chance to re-grow, it can never become what it was. Such regenerated jungles have an entirely different character. Many of the plants and animals in the original forest become extinct, and trees and other plants that have evolved to grow in the dark, humid environment of the jungle simply cannot behave naturally when they find themselves having to regenerate out in the open. Even if only small parcels of land throughout an area are destroyed, these remnants change in due course. Birds and other animals cannot cross from one to another, so plants are not pollinated, seeds are not dispersed by the animals, and the plants around the edges are not surrounded by the high jungle humidity which they need to grow properly. As a result the remnants slowly become degraded.

workers and provide them with shops and places of entertainment. To service the plant and the community 2,800 miles (4,500 km) of roads have been built for the 700 vehicles, and a 26 mile (42 km) railway. Each day the plant burns 2,000 tons of wood to produce the 55 megawatts of power needed to turn out, every 24 hours, about 1,000 tons of bleached pulp, which earn about £300,000. As part of the whole scene, and as visualised by its creator from the beginning, there is an attendant rice-growing enterprise. The original idea was that enough rice could be grown to feed Brazil, and the plant is indeed producing very large quantities of rice each year. The whole Jari enterprise takes up 0.03 per cent of the Amazon jungle

The rainforest tries to get its own back of course and $5 m a year is spent simply trying to keep it at bay, but it is a sad, sterile place where wildlife is sparse and no birds sing in the imported trees.

From the air above the Amazon rainforest one can see the scale of projects like this or the Trans-Amazon Highway which is a wide red scar hundreds of miles long right through the middle of Brazil. The destruction involved is enormous.

About a hundred years ago the Frenchman Ferdinand de Lesseps began the work which was going to end up as the Panama Canal. At the time Panama belonged to Colombia. De Lesseps had an awful time and in the end returned to France without achieving very much, where he died in poverty and disgrace. In 1903 Panama achieved independence from Colombia and America decided to take over from de Lesseps. The country negotiated with the government of the newly independent Panama for rights over what was to be known as the Canal Zone. Work was recommenced on the canal and by 1914 it was completed at a cost of $387 m. It was an extraordinary achievement and cut 9,000 miles from the sea journey between New York and San Francisco. It has proved invaluable since the beginning, and is still used by many large ships that are cosseted and helped through the narrow locks by toytown tugs on either bank, though if you stand beside one it no longer looks as though it is from toytown.

Today there are considerable doubts about the future of the canal because in recent years large tracts of forest on either bank have been logged, with the inevitable result that rain has started to erode the banks which have been ending up in the bottom of the canal. This is not just a matter of a few tons of soil here and there; it is happening for miles. Many experts say that before long the whole thing will no longer be navigable and that the cost of solving the problem will be prohibitive. Would it not be strange if a few decades after the canal was completed, with all

(OPPOSITE)
As soon as a tree dies, light is let into the depths of the forest and trees shoot up. Only those that grow fastest towards the light will survive (*Adrian Warren*)

■

On 27 November 1988 Thailand's Foreign Minister, Siddhi Savetsila, appealed to the rest of the world to help his country in the aftermath of the worst floods for forty years which had led to the deaths of 232 people. In addition, hundreds were missing and about 250,000 had been left homeless.

Government officials blamed illegal logging for the floods. The subsequent rains had stripped the soil from the hillsides, and the resulting mud and water had devastated entire villages in the south of the country.

The deputy Minister of the Interior commented, during a visit to the area, 'Nature has delivered its message to the entire nation that it can no longer take the rape and plunder that those illegal poachers levelled on it.'

WHAT HAPPENS WHEN RAINFORESTS DISAPPEAR?

NO ONE KNOWS EXACTLY what is going to happen to the world if all our rainforests disappear, but by doing their sums and examining computer predictions scientists have come up with all sorts of theories and there now seems little doubt that most of these predictions will come to pass if we carry on destroying the forests in the way we are now, and most scientists, after years of haggling and arguing about unimportant academic protocols, nowadays seem to be pretty much agreed. Indeed, all of us are already beginning to notice changes taking place and, whereas some of these developments might be due to other manmade causes, the changes are all so often closely linked with each other that it is difficult to separate them.

The first and most obvious thing that will happen when the jungles have gone is that all the animals and plants that lived in them will have disappeared for ever. When someone is interested in conservation and moves amongst people who are also interested in conservation it begins to seem that everyone is. It is

Victorian explorers referred to jungles as green hells. They are far less threatening than a city, and infinitely more beautiful.

∎

A mother and her baby rest in a hammock made from jungle plants. Until recently, all this family's needs were supplied by the forest (*Adrian Warren*)

(OVERLEAF)
The rivers and creeks of Amazonia serve the area as highways. During the rainy season, the flow of water increases enormously and fallen leaves and branches are swept along on the flood (*Adrian Warren*)

∎

only when he or she moves outside these circles that it is brought home that most people in the world do not give a damn about the subject. It is quite extraordinary that in this day and age, when you would think that nobody could fail to be aware of the environmental problems facing us, most are completely oblivious to them. Surely everybody must know that giant pandas are endangered? There seems to be something about pandas just about every week in the press or on television, and yet ordinary intelligent people have expressed surprise when I have told them. Perhaps the reason for this is that pandas live on the other side of the world and the fate of these attractive animals has nothing to do with their lives, and one can certainly comprehend this point of view.

Rainforests are different because, when they disappear, all our lives are going to be affected adversely, and if we continue abusing them the way we are doing this is going to happen far sooner than anyone thinks. As we have seen, an enormous number of things that we nowadays take for granted came originally from the jungles of the world. We have also looked at the fact that we have only examined a tiny fraction of 1 per cent of the plants and animals to see what might be of use to us. If we destroy them all before we have a chance to do at least this basic research, it will be too late to regret it afterwards.

There must be plants in the jungles that could be used to make medicines that would cure many of our problems. There must be plants that we could cultivate as food crops. Only recently, when we have discovered that fossil fuels are not going to last much longer and we are going to run out of petrol for our cars, someone has found that suitable alternatives can be produced from certain plants. Sugar cane was one of them and, as I write, in today's newspaper it is suggested that oilseed rape could be used for the same thing. Just imagine how many plants there are in the rainforest that might also be of use.

Such an argument is easy enough for anyone to understand and, when I say that animals might disappear before we can explore their potential as well, I do not mean their consumption for food or medicine, but very frequently scientists looking at particular animals discover a fact of interest by accident that might benefit us. If we discover why or how an animal does something we can relate it to the way the same thing happens in human beings. The untapped potential of the jungles is so vast that their disappearance before we can research them is frightening. The vast store of genes can be matched nowhere else on earth.

The next point to bear in mind is that most of the rainforest destruction is caused by burning. Until fifty years ago all the fires in the world were not enough to make any difference on a global scale, though we should remember that until then London used to suffer from the most dreadful smog due to the coal burnt in that city. Nowadays the picture is completely different. There is not a single city in the world where cars are not rushing about burning petrol or diesel fuel, and the fumes drift up into the air. In Brazil and other countries in South and Central America the smoke from fires burning the jungle is sometimes so thick that great palls of it drift for miles. The same is happening everywhere. In Thailand, even in protected forests, the smoke of a dozen fires can be observed on any day just by turning through 360 degrees. In Malaysia, Africa and Indonesia the story is the same. Each year we are burning rainforest at the rate of 1.2 billion acres (50 million hectares) a year—that is nearly a million hectares every week, or a football pitch a minute, which is a horrifying statistic.

The fumes from the cars and the burning forests are already causing us problems. Everybody has heard of the greenhouse effect. The atmosphere is warming up slowly but not so slowly that we cannot notice. If this continues various things are going to happen, of which perhaps the most dramatic will be that the polar ice will melt, and that means that the level of the seas is going to rise. It does not take much thought to realise that

Gorillas are rare and protected jungle animals. In 1984 applications were made by three American zoos to import seven gorillas from Cameroon; the applications were refused on 9 April 1984.

Later, on 8 June, all seven animals were imported into Holland, bought by the Foundation Netherlands National IUCN Committee for deposit on breeding loan at the Burgers Zoo in Arnhem. The Management Authority of the Convention on International Trade in Endangered Species permitted the importation for breeding purposes provided that the animals were used only for breeding and for education; that no purchase price was paid, but only certain unavoidable expenses; and that the gorillas remained available for an educational project inside Cameroon or for breeding within the framework of the international studbook.

Half of the expenses paid went to the government of Cameroon in export fees.

A Waorani hunter returns with his prey. He lives entirely off the jungle in the Cononaco region of Ecuador (*Adrian Warren*)

∎

Originally Japan made most of its cardboard packaging for electronic equipment from wood chips from the United States, but in recent years there have been far fewer new houses built, with the result that waste chips are no longer available in the required quantities.

The shortfall is produced from the jungle of places like Madang on the north coast of Papua New Guinea, where huge machines, the latest technological marvels, tear the forest to pieces. The machines weight 15 tonnes and have 8 ft (2.4 m) cutting discs with eight blades, which revolve 320 times a minute in order to cut trees into chips half the size of a matchbox. More than 200 species of trees can be gobbled up by these machines which are busy clearing a concession measuring 320 square miles (515 km²).

many of the world's capital cities are built at sea level because they started life as trading ports that needed harbours and ships. If the melting of the ice caps raised the water levels by only a metre, and of all the current estimates that is very conservative, just think how many cities would no longer exist.

Another thing that is happening as a result of all the fires is that levels of carbon monoxide and carbon dioxide in the air are going up. At one time the enormous acreage of trees in the world used to recycle the carbon monoxide as part of the normal process of transpiration, returning oxygen to the atmosphere. Nowadays the trees that are left are having a job keeping up. As if that were not enough, other toxic gases in the air from these and other sources are now causing acid rain. What happens is that hydrogen, oxygen and sulphur are released into the air, where they combine to form sulphuric acid. When it rains the sulphuric acid falls onto buildings and trees and begins to destroy them. Buildings in many of the world's cities are now suffering from acid rain damage, and trees that have not burnt down are beginning to die as a result of the same contamination.

Weather patterns are changing too, and the consensus of informed opinion is that this too is a direct result of destruction of the forest. Ever since the beginning of time the great humidity of the big forest masses has meant that the heat has taken the moisture vertically into the air above them and the resulting atmospheric pressure has resulted in weather patterns that have remained consistent over the centuries. Today the forests are going and the weather is changing, as everyone must have noticed. Who knows what the end results of this are going to be? In the meantime it throws the life cycles of plants and animals into disarray, and from our point of view that could ultimately mean problems with crops, and breeding cycles of domestic animals, and difficulties all round for farmers.

In the countries in which they are still to be found, the people who live in and around the forests are disappearing as well. Their homes, their environments and their life styles are vanishing. Their cultures are being eroded and not being replaced with anything else of equal value. What can a man of fifty who has spent his entire life living by boiling parts of certain trees and shooting fish with a bow and arrow do in the modern world? Many of them in despair turn to the new towns to try and earn a living without the necessary skills or the money to put up to build a business.

It is not only the aborigine in the fast-disappearing remnants of Australia's forest who will suffer; nor will the Indian from the Amazon be the only one to watch his home and life disappear. The destruction of the forests is going to affect you

Though there is often legislation to prevent destruction of an environment in Third World countries, it is commonly flouted openly. In the New World countries where rainforest is to be found, only in Costa Rica, a progressive, stable and democratic country, is there a conservation policy that works, though it must be said that much destruction had already been wrought before the current situation was arrived at.

In Panama the loss of the forests has been very severe, so much so that there is a real danger that the Panama Canal will no longer be able to function within a few years. New roads are opening up much of the interior, and whilst the roads themselves cause much damage, they also leave the immediate area accessible to even more exploitation.

The Amazon rainforest covers Brazil, Colombia, Venezuela, Bolivia, Peru and the three Guyanas. This massive area represents 54 per cent of the world's rainforest and contains about 900 tonnes of living plants per hectare. Altogether it contains the largest collection of living plant and animal species in the world.

THE RAINFORESTS OF SOUTH AMERICA.

Bolivia — As yet there is not too much exploitation of the forest, but it is beginning.
Brazil — Suffering badly for a variety of reasons. Parts of the west are as yet undisturbed due to inaccessibility.
Colombia — About one third forested, mostly in the south.
Ecuador — Much of the rainforest along the Pacific has already disappeared. Exploration for oil, and to an extent agriculture, are putting pressure on Ecuador's Amazon forest.
French Guiana — Virtually all the population live along the coastal strip and as yet the forest is almost untouched.
Guyana — Although the forests are comparatively untouched, exploitation is increasing.
Peru — There are still vast areas of undisturbed rainforest.
Surinam — Little damage has yet been done to the forests. There are several parks and reserves. This was one of the first countries to dam and flood an area of forest.
Venezuela — A large tract in the south of the country is still pretty well intact, though in the north there is a fair bit of damage.

THE RAINFORESTS OF THE CARIBBEAN AND CENTRAL AMERICA.

Most islands have lost much of their original forests but small, decreasing areas can be found on some islands such as the Dominican Republic, Puerto Rico, Trinidad and Tobago.
Much central American forest has disappeared, mainly due to cattle ranching and fruit farms.
Belize — There is a still considerable amount of virgin forest, but exploitation is beginning to be felt.
Costa Rica — The national parks represent the best of the forest to be seen.
Guatemala — Small areas are still to be found in the north-eastern Peten region.
Honduras — The Mosquitia forest in the east is still fairly intact, due to the unstable political situation in Central America.
Mexico — The country's last forest on the border of Guatemala is fast disappearing as timber and cattle concerns move in.
Nicaragua — Some small forests are left, because the war has made exploitation an uncertain business.
Panama — What forest is left is fast disappearing and is unlikely to last much longer.

THE RAINFORESTS OF AFRICA.

Angola — There is a small area of rainforest in the north of the country.
Benin — Three-quarters of the original forest remains, but the population is growing fast.
Cameroon — Very large tracts of this magnificent forest are disappearing beneath timber concessions, cattle ranches and slash and burn economies. Conservation of what is left

is now under way.
Central African Republic — There are untouched rainforests in the south, which, because of the poor economy, are likely to stay this way.

Equatorial Guinea — The country is almost completely forested, and likely to remain that way.

Gabon — Though the country is almost completely forested, exploitation is now under way.

Ghana — Only a very little remains. The rest has almost completely disappeared in the last 25 years.

Guinea — There is still a small area of forest remaining.

Ivory Coast — Almost all the forest has disappeared. Pressures on what remains are intense.

Liberia — Very little forest remains.

Madagascar — Only a small area of the original forest in the east remains.

Nigeria — Most forest has been logged out, and what is left is likely to disappear soon.

Rwanda — Some forest remains.

Sierra Leone — Very little of the forest remains undisturbed by cultivators.

Zaire — Contains Africa's largest rainforest, which is nearly 10 per cent of the world total. While much remains undamaged, it is beginning to be exploited.

THE RAINFORESTS OF ASIA.

Bangladesh — There is a narrow belt of rainforest around Chittagong which is exploited extensively by the hill tribes.

Brunei — Pretty well covered in rainforest, much of it undisturbed. Unlike many neighbouring countries, the pressure on the forest is not great since much of the country's foreign currency comes from oil revenue.

Burma — Much of the country is forested, and because of the xenophobic communist government policies of the last 40 years there has been little trade with the outside world. Consequently there has been little disturbance.

China — There are rainforests along the south which are badly disturbed, though there are a few reserves.

India — There are still largish patches of forest that are disappearing, but slowly.

Indonesia — This country of many islands contains the largest rainforest in Asia (about 10 per cent of the world total). It is disappearing at an alarming rate due to encouragement of logging practices.

Kampuchea — Some areas of rainforest survive, and are likely to do so until peace and prosperity return to the country.

Malaysia — Formerly well covered by rainforest. The government actively encourages logging, and what is left will soon disappear.

Papua New Guinea — As yet still extensively covered by rainforest, as much is inaccessible on the sides of mountains. Some foresting goes on.

Philippines — Only a third of the original forest remains, and that is not likely to last very long.

Sri Lanka — Some forest remains, largely disrupted by logging operations.

Thailand — Some forest remains in this most beautiful of countries, but despite reserves and protective legislation it is disappearing fast.

Vietnam — The rainforests have been virtually destroyed, partly due to the American use of the defoliant Agent Orange during the Vietnam War. A replanting operation is currently taking place. The country is replanting 500 million trees.

THE RAINFORESTS OF AUSTRALIA AND THE PACIFIC ISLANDS.

Some small areas remain along the coast of Queensland, but they are unlikely to remain undisturbed for long. Logging is already taking place. Tasmania is contantly fighting to save what is left from commercial concerns and uncaring politicians.

Some Pacific islands contain small areas of rainforest. Much of that on Fiji has been granted to logging concessions. Three quarters of the Solomon Islands forests remain because the slopes on which they are found make access for machinery impracticable.

In the Malaysian state of Sarawak on the island of Borneo live a group of Dayaks known as the Penan. As is happening all over the world where people live in forests, their homes are disappearing in front of the giant logging machines.

The Penan, however, unlike many other people in this situation, refused to take it lying down, and in 1987 the loggers in the camps between Tutoh and Limbang had to be very careful indeed. The Penan had dug in their heels and refused to let any logging take place. The loggers could see no sign of the Penan but they knew that behind every tree there lurked men with blowpipes. All the roads had been blocked and work was at a standstill.

The Malaysian government has imposed a blackout on news from the area and no one knows what is happening at the moment. But any action by Malaysia against the Penan is going to have to be taken in the face of world disapproval.

and it is going to affect me as it has already affected the starving people of Ethiopia and Sudan, areas that were clothed in trees in days gone by. It is also going to affect the pampered businesspeople sitting in their air-conditioned offices in the financial centres of the world who are putting money and expertise into forest destruction, and taking the profit out of it. They might not realise it, or they may choose to ignore the signs and the warnings, but there is no way of escaping the consequences if we do not stop this nonsense, and stop it now.

For a quarter of a century conservationists have been warning of what is happening, only to be ignored. Today, thank goodness, companies and politicians are beginning to be stirred out of their inertia. This can only be a good thing so long as they actually do something about it now. If they let ten years pass while they wait for yet more unnecessary reports it will be too late. I cannot understand the thinking behind the procrastination. Surely the thing to do is to say, 'Look, there is some evidence that rainforest destruction might be doing all this. Stop it now and then do the research. We can always start again if it turns out we were wrong.' As it is, the companies and the politicans are suddenly turning green for the most cynical, exploitative reasons, not because they think it actually matters. A politician feels she will attract more votes if she tells us she has always been a friend of the earth. A food manufacturer feels he will sell more of his product to all these nuts if he shows he cares as much as they do. Very few do it because it matters, though there are some noble exceptions, such as Anita Roddick and her chain of Body Shops, and Katherine Hammnett the fashion designer.

The sad thing is that all this destruction of our most important and commercially viable assets is completely unnecesssary. Who was it who said that nature abhors a vacuum? In the same spirit I am sure that powerful businesspeople abhor anything that is not producing money. A while ago a farmer on television was justifying his destruction of a medieval flower meadow in the face of considerable protest from the conservation movement. Look at it now, he exclaimed. It was a mess of scrub and bushes and just see how I have tidied it up. I am sure the same peculiar mentality affects those people whose lives are ruled by account sheets and lists of figures.

The trouble in the past has often been that the World Bank and other major financial institutions have been only too happy to lend money to countries for schemes that have been environmentally damaging. There were huge profits apparently to be made from the loans so they were approved without thought of the damage they would be responsible for. Today such money markets are far less inclined to lend money for this

(OPPOSITE)

A leader of the Penan tribe contemplates a future without a forest as loggers tear the jungle to pieces around his home (*CAP/Third World/Survival International*)

■

One of the difficulties about our losing rain-forests before we have discovered all there is to know about them is that we may lose for ever a whole host of commodities that might be useful to man. And we would never know.

About 1.7 million species of animal have so far been described scientifically. About 1.5 million of these are from temperate regions, which is not to say that there are only a few in the tropics, but rather that the temperate regions have been far more extensively investi-gated.

In fact, it has been calculated that there might be at least 3 million species in the tropics alone, and there are even suggestions that throughout the world the total number of species, if only we knew them all, might be 10 million.

A little Waorani girl is happy to show off some of the few
things in her life not obtained from the forest (*Adrian Warren*)

(LEFT)
Following a death, many forest people burn their huts and move on to a new site (*Adrian Warren*) ■

sort of project. The reasons are twofold. First, there is so much public concern about rainforest destruction, and about all sorts of other environmentally damaging schemes, that banks are far more cagey about them. The second reason is that it has emerged over the years that many of the countries that borrowed the money in the first place are completely unable to repay it, even if they want to. Their economies are just not buoyant enough, and Brazil for example spends 40 per cent of its annual income in simply servicing its loans.

Public concern over lending money to environmentally damaging schemes has mounted to such an extent over the last ten years or so that many investors no longer wish to put their money into companies that are involved with such projects. Consequently a completely new animal has appeared in the world of finance. Nowadays there are unit trust companies which ensure that investors' money is only put into those concerns which are environmentally sound. Some of these unit trusts are only concerned with matters that are strictly environmental. Others work with a wider brief and refuse to have anything to do with companies or countries that also have a bad reputation in fields of racial prejudice, human rights and so on. Investments like this have been becoming very popular recently and the number of firms offering such options is increasing all the time.

Australian conservationists are having to fight every inch of the way against some strange ideas. In Queensland, for example, the state premier Sir Joh Bjelke-Petersen has suggested that life might be easier for swimmers if all the crocodiles were captured and put into zoos. Anyone who knows anything about animals or conservation has enjoyed what they thought could only be a joke, but the man appears to be serious, and the scheme might yet take place.

WHO CAUSES THE DESTRUCTION?

Once trees have been removed, the bare soil and the rest of the forest is very vulnerable. At the following rains any topsoil is eroded, taking with it trees growing lower down the hill. Before long this small hole in the jungle has become a large area of bare hillside (*David Potter*)

■

Rubberwood is a sustainable tropical timber that is largely ignored by the trade. It can be used for crates, pallets, door thresholds, window frames, furniture carcases, and fruit bowls.

VIRTUALLY ALL HOUSEHOLD FURNITURE is either veneered with teak or some other forest timber, or actually made from the stuff completely. But the situation is beginning to change and nowadays there is plenty of good furniture around that is made from oak and other temperate hardwoods. That was not the case until recently, and even today one can look through furniture catalogues and watch advertisements on television which proudly proclaim a company's use of rainforest hardwood.

Some little time ago the conservation organisation Friends of the Earth produced a book entitled *The Good Wood Guide*. It seemed an excellent idea at the time as it listed companies throughout Britain that dealt in wooden items. These firms were divided into those who were aware of the problems of rainforest destruction and therefore did not use any timber from these sources, those that did but were trying to limit their imports, and those that, frankly, did not give a damn. There was an immediate furore. The timber trade raised its collective hackles and mumbled meaningless platitudes, and the dealers who were listed under the section for 'Baddies' huffed and puffed likewise. One of the aims of the exercise was to award a seal of approval to companies that did not contribute to rainforest destruction, but I have not since then seen any sign of it. I feel that FOE went about the whole thing in a rather insensitive fashion and promptly put everyone's back up unnecessarily but, that said, there is no doubt at all that the timber trade is extraordinarily lethargic about the whole business. Even some importers (and one person at the headquarters of the Timber Trade Association who insisted on not being named) admit quite frankly that there is terrific inertia to overcome within the business and until it is compelled to do something about it there is unlikely to be any change.

Certain factors may force their hand. One is that some countries that supply the timber are now realising that their stocks are disappearing fast and that if they are to retain any credibility in the eyes of the world as being caring nations they are going to have to do something about it. Indonesia for example has now banned the export of ramin, a wood that has been used for all sorts of things like broom handles. Indonesia was previously the major supplier of this species of timber.

But while you and I continue to demand turned rosewood fruit bowls and teak coffee tables, little is going to change. Much of the destruction is a direct result of the countries of origin wanting to pay off the crippling international loans with which they have saddled themselves. They cannot hope to do this by selling the trees for the timber; there just are not enough of them. But by clearing the jungle they can start mining for valuable minerals. In addition they are building hydro-electric dams to provide cheap electricity for their industries. This means flooding whole valleys, and at the moment in Brazil there are over a hundred such schemes in operation. Vast tracts of forest are disappearing in this fashion. We looked earlier at the Jari pulpwood scheme, and other projects like it are bringing valuable foreign currency to the host countries. One plant, again in Brazil, makes steel for Japanese cars. Thousands upon thousands of tons of rainforest timber are being burnt each year to produce charcoal that can be used in the manufacture of steel. Why? Because you and I want the latest Japanese cars.

And why are the empty spaces being turned into cattle ranches? Because you and I want hamburgers by the ton. The answer to the worldwide problem is to persuade the ultimate consumers not to insist on commodities that exacerbate it, for it is no use hoping that companies will voluntarily stop despoiling the jungles. On the other hand it is easy to understand a poor, Third World country full of what to it seems useless rainforest selling rights to exploit it to foreign firms.

Some time ago I was talking to a man in Bangkok who is the biggest animal dealer in Thailand. He is also an astute businessman who has commercial interests in all sorts of other areas. On this occasion, while I was having lunch in his house, we were talking about the need for conservation and how to make it work. He is a superb naturalist and the first person to agree that many species of animal are disappearing and should be conserved. While he is still responsible for taking plenty of animals out of the wild, he is trying to breed as many species as he can and has set up a variety of breeding programmes. Recently the Thai government had brought in legislation banning the trade in greater hill mynahs except under strict quotas. This quota system is open to all sorts of abuse, whatever

The indri, a Madagascan lemur. These delightful primates fill the niche that is occupied elsewhere by monkeys (there are no monkeys in Madagascar) (*Adrian Warren*)

One of Mexico's leading ecologists, Gabriel Quadri, has stated publicly that the growth of cattle ranching in Mexico is causing the systematic destruction of the country's rainforest, and that the authorities are not doing enough to save what is left. Senor Quadri insists that 37 million acres (14.9 million hectares) have gone in the last 15 years alone.

He says that 'nobody in the government cares about saving them'. On the contrary, the government have just established an under-ministry of cattle farming, but there is no ministry to protect the rainforests.

On the other hand, President Carlos Salinas de Gortari has promised protection for the Chiapas forests of the state of Lacandon. He made this promise a week after taking office in December 1988.

Dani tribesmen outside their hut in Irian Jaya, Indonesia. Everyday costume for men includes penis sheaths. Fruit and vegetables have been collected for the next meal (*Adrian Arbib*)

■

In 1986 *The Observer* reported how in Sarawak on the island of Borneo the Samling Timber company had bought forests by giving 2000 Malaysian dollars to 12 longhouses. This sum amounted to the price of two bottles of beer for each member of the community.

Since then this company and others have managed to extract about a third of Sarawak's forest — about 6.9 million acres (2.8 million hectares). Some of the local people have been induced to work for the logging companies, but a logger in Sarawak is 21 times more likely to have a serious accident than a logger in Canada.

Marcus Colchester, of Survival International, points out that when he left in 1987 the whole area surrounding the Penan Islands was sealed off by armed police.

and more friendly and she told me her story. She had started life in a village in south-western India on the edge of the forest where her family farmed a small plot, never doing well, but always managing to scratch a living from one season to the next. The great problem in their lives was trying to pay off the enormous debts that accrued with the local moneylender, who charged an exorbitant rate of interest. The difficulty in such a situation is the servicing of the debt and the only way is often to take out yet another debt knowing perfectly well that it would only increase the borrower's difficulties. However, there was always next year's crop—if it was a good one and could be sold at a profit a fair part of the money owing could be cleared.

This family's really hard times had started forty years previously when the old lady was a young bride. One year the monsoon was late and the crops failed and there was nothing anybody could do except watch the carefully nurtured seedlings wilt and die, and all that could be done was to take out yet another loan from the hated moneylender against the income from the following year's crops.

In theory this should have worked but twelve months later the rains were late again and once more there was no crop. This time, as the family despairingly watched the small plants grow yellow, the woman's husband felt that he could not go on like this without taking some other steps to earn enough to keep his family and, after considerable discussion with every member of his extended family, he set off for Bombay to see what he could find. After a short unsuccessful time in that city during which he made a few rupees hauling fish to Crawford Market on the enormously long bamboo barrows that are used for the purpose, a friend of his who worked in the bird market suggested that the two of them travel to Calcutta where, he had heard, pickings were easier to come by. Things could not be much worse where they were and the two men eventually made the decision and, sending word to his family that he would contact them again when he got to Calcutta and found work, the woman's husband and his friend set off full of hope for Bori Bunder, the extraordinary, flamboyant railway station that looks as though a mad architect has tried to redesign the Natural History Museum in London.

They could not possibly afford the train fare so they did what every poor Indian does in these circumstances: they waited until the very last moment and as the train started to move they dived onto any foothold they could find on the outside of one of the already packed-to-bursting third-class carriages. Two miserable days followed, surviving on as little food as they could, jumping off the train when they felt threatened by ticket inspectors, and jamming themselves into any corner they could

find when the train was on the move. Seasoned travellers could have told them that there was not much to fear from ticket inspectors in third-class accommodation since these carriages are so packed that one could not have made his way along them if he had wanted to.

Finally, the two exhausted youths arrived at Howrah, the huge, filthy, noisy station that serves Calcutta. They had almost no money, no work, nowhere to go, and no idea of the geography of the place, but eventually, after talking to other people, they discovered that Howrah is on the west bank of the River Hooghly, and that the city itself is on the other side. They set off to cross the huge Meccano edifice that is Howrah Bridge.

The old woman's husband thought he had been badly off in his village, and then he discovered that he was even poorer in Bombay. In Calcutta he found what real poverty meant and for five years he earned a few annas here and a few annas there as a porter, as a ricksaw puller briefly until he was involved in an accident and broke a foot, as a shoe shine wallah and as anything else that would pay any money at all. Every scrap of his earnings he sent back home to his family, and he existed in the meantime by scavenging round the food markets and the back of hotels and restaurants for any food that had been thrown out as inedible, and if you know Calcutta you will know just how bad things must have been.

In time things did improve and he managed to make what seemed a fortune after his previous bad luck, as an unofficial basket wallah at New Market. Basket wallahs are a strange breed that hang around outside a bazaar and accost any customers entering the place. If their luck is in they persuade the customer to let them carry all her purchases until she returns to her car or taxi, and in India, where anyone of any status refuses to demean themselves with tasks they consider to be beneath them, basket wallahs find a surprising number of customers. For this service they are paid a minuscule fee. They are however, supposed to be licensed and official basket wallahs sport an armband bearing their number. Nowadays, most of the unlicensed ones have disappeared but at that time there were plenty of them. They had to keep out of the way of the market inspector who would throw them out if he saw them touting for business, though the fear of ejection disappeared once they had found a customer as the inspector would demand a proportion of the fee.

As a basket wallah the young man managed to send regular, comparatively large amounts back to his family and even maintain a standard of living that was acceptable compared to his previous existence. He lived on the pavement near New Market, and his particular patch was regarded as inviolate by all the other street dwellers. Nevertheless it was a lonely life and he

Tam Dalyell, the British Labour Member of Parliament, told a crowd of listeners at Altamira in Brazil that the country ought to stop building dams and thereby destroying large tracts of rainforest, and '... instead of building the Xingu River dam it should build safe, less destructive nuclear power plants.' He asked, 'Isn't this a better alternative than flooding the Amazon forest and creating a biological holocaust?'

The world's smallest bird, the bee hummingbird, is about the size of a bumble bee, 2¼ in (5.7cm) long. It weighs less than two grams.

By no means every hunting expedition is successful, but this hunter is delighted to have secured two monkeys by using his blowpipe loaded with poison-tipped darts (Adrian Warren)

Baskets are invaluable and come in all sizes. The forest provides materials to make them, including dyes (*Adrian Warren*)

■

In June 1989 a British national newspaper revealed that Barclays Bank had been involved in cattle ranching operations in Brazil which had resulted in the destruction of half a million acres (200,000 hectares) of rainforest.

As soon as he heard this, the chairman of Barclays, John Quinton, ordered the sale of Barclays' shares in the ranches which it had held through its half ownership of BCN Barclays Banco de Investimento SA. This particular bank owned the cattle ranches in conjunction with the Condes, one of Brazil's wealthiest families, and the Banco Nacional do Brasil.

John Quinton is quoted as saying that the company had become involved in something that was not in accordance with its commercial policy, nor with its ecological interests.

missed his wife and the small son he had almost forgotten, so he visited a letter writer and got him to write to his wife suggesting she came and join him, and to his delight she did, bringing their son with her, and the young family set up their home on the pavement.

For a while things did not go too badly but then the hard times began again and on this occasion things went from bad to worse. When the boy became ill and their new baby also caught the same infection there was no money for the parents to buy treatment of any sort for their children and in desperation the father sold some blood to a clinic. That helped a little, but in time he was having to do this regularly until in the end the clinics refused to accept him any more as a donor. He was too weak and too ill, and just kept returning too frequently. One day at one of these clinics someone asked him why he did not sell his bones.

This sounded terrifying and he did not want to imagine how anyone could extract his bones without killing him first, and in any case he asked, why would anyone want his bones? It was explained to him that skeletons were in demand by foreign medical schools for teaching purposes, and there was no question of anyone killing him for his bones. They would not be required until his death.

Seeing this as the only option open to him he made his way to the address he had been given and was interviewed by a fat Bengali who finally agreed to buy his skeleton. He was paid a third of the cost of the purchase at the time, and was told that he could claim a further third a year later if he lived that long. The final third would be paid to his widow on collection after his death. The unhappy man agreed. Later he told his wife, shuddering at the memory of the Bengali's workplace where men toiled in the steam and smell arising from huge vats where they boiled all the muscle and other soft tissues from the bones of what had been men and women a few days previously. He also told of the ornaments made from bones that he had seen in the fat proprietor's office. He survived to collect the second instalment of the money a year later but the family's situation got no better and eventually the man died and in time the children moved away to try and make a better living for themselves, leaving the widow to eke out the rest of her days on the pavements of Calcutta where she was when I first came to know her.

I dearly wanted to help but I had no idea how she would react if I offered her money since she had never asked for it. How she retained her sanity and sense of humour I shall never know, but her biography which was told in short instalments over several weeks was always related in humorous fashion

A young palm tree grows a large leaf to catch every scrap of light in an attempt to beat its neighbours to the top (*Adrian Warren*)

interspersed with smiles. One day when I went to visit the old woman I made sure that before I left I dropped a 5 rupee note on the pavement and failed to notice when I left. Five rupees is not much, only 20–30p at the time, but to her it must have been an appreciable sum.

The next day as I approached my friend she held out the note and told me that I must have dropped it. Can you imagine the mental struggle she must have been through before returning it to me? I told her that I had not lost 5 rupees and suggested that the sensible thing to do would be to hang on to it. I am sure she did not believe me but she did as I suggested. Every few days after that I would repeat the gesture. She had understood, and did not offer to return the money again and the system worked well for both of us.

When I was about to leave India I went to see my old lady for the last time. I told her I was leaving and that I wished her happiness for the future. I had on me about £30 in Indian currency. I kept £5 worth for anything I might need at the airport before I left and held out the remainder. I explained that I had bought all I wanted to in India and that I would be unable to change the remainder into sterling. I would be pleased if she would have it. In the end she agreed to take it. It was one of the most moving moments of my life. She told me that she had never seen so much money and thought that it probably equalled everything that she had previously earned throughout her lifetime. If I really had no use for it, she told me, she would

The 'greenhouse effect' is a term commonly used these days, but it is perhaps not understood by a lot of people.

Carbon dioxide is a common gas. The bubbles in fizzy drinks are carbon dioxide which is also an important gas in the earth's atmosphere, even though it only amounts to 0.03 per cent of the total.

When the rays of the sun meet the outer surface of the earth's atmosphere most of them are reflected back into space. However, within the last century or so the carbon dioxide levels in the atmosphere have been increasing. At the time of the Industrial Revol-ution we began to burn fossil fuels in huge quantities for the first time. The gases released from this combustion meant that an ever increasing amount of the sun's energy was now able to be absorbed by the atmosphere rather than bouncing off it. The increased energy reaching the surface of our planet has been slowly warming it until the difference has now become crucial.

Much of the increased carbon dioxide comes from the burning of petrol in cars and other sources, but because we are now burning enormous tracts of rainforest, the gas from that operation is also making a significant difference to the carbon dioxide level in the atmosphere.

In 1850 there were 265 parts per million of carbon dioxide in the air. Today the figure is about 340, and if we continue as we are doing, it could reach 600 by the year 2050. This will result in the average temperature of the earth rising by 3 degrees Centigrade. Although not much difference would be noticed at the equator, the polar regions would be about 7 degrees warmer, causing the ice caps to begin to melt, which in turn would raise the sea level, with all that that implies.

be happy to make use of it. I gave it to her, said goodbye and went away. I never saw her again.

Three years ago I went past the same spot deliberately when I was in Calcutta but not surprisingly the old lady was not there. One cold night she must have died, alone, uncared for and unloved.

That story takes place all over the world every year as people of the rainforests are losing their homes and their livelihoods, driven into an uncaring world where they have no place. It is easy to forget such people, living as they do on the other side of the world where we can neither see them nor hear their pleas for help but, if the world responded to the plight of the starving Ethiopians and Sudanese, surely it makes sense to think seriously about the problem of the rainforests, which is destroying many adults and children around the world and, if the situation is allowed to continue, might very well be the death of us as well?

Some organisations that are working towards the conservation of rainforests ask for money to buy up tracts of jungle to be managed, and this is certainly one thing that can be done, but the most important thing of all does not need us to commit a single penny of our income. All we need to do is to ensure that we do not buy any rainforest products, to spread the word so that our friends do not either, and to insist that no investments we make in companies are supporting the sort of businesses that are involved in schemes contributing to the loss of our forests.

WHAT ARE THE ALTERNATIVES?

THE ONLY SENSIBLE WAY to end the destruction of all the remaining rainforest is to persuade everyone concerned that the jungles are worth more money left where they are. But we will not persuade anyone unless we make sure that the statement is true, and there is no doubt that the answer lies in the hands of the developed countries.

The governments of Indonesia, Malaysia and Brazil have expressed their anger at what they see as interference in their own internal affairs, when environmental arguments about rainforest have been levelled at them by people from abroad. Narrow-minded though this response may be, it is perfectly understandable. A financially attractive alternative must be presented to them, and today there are all sorts of ways this can be done.

Brazil has suggested in anger that if, as everyone else says, tropical forests such as the Amazon jungle are important to the rest of the world in keeping the balance of atmospheric gases stable and the climate as it is now, then the world in general ought to be willing to put its money where its mouth is and pay Brazil for the service.

A version of this idea is now a real possibility. It has been suggested that the most sensible way out of the situation is for countries with rainforests who are unable to repay their foreign debts to agree instead to what have come to be known as debt-for-nature swaps. The situation has arisen where lenders are beginning to realise that the chance of getting back their money is becoming more remote by the day; so what they do is to put the debt up for sale in the financial markets at the best price they can get, and write the rest off to experience. Conservation bodies and others can buy these debts at an advantageous price, freeing the country from the obligation to continue paying. In

This ring-tailed lemur is soaking up the morning sun (*Adrian Warren*)

(OPPOSITE)
At dawn a forest looks as though it is on fire, but it is only mist rising from the trees (*David Potter*)
■

Sunsets do not last long in the tropics, but they are often magnificent (*Adrian Warren*)

(OVERLEAF)
Forests like this one in Rwanda, Africa, play an essential part in regulating the levels of gases in the atmosphere, and thus the climates and weather of the world (*Adrian Warren*)

■

Each year Africa provides 60 million cubic metres of industrial wood and 380 million cubic metres of fuel wood, Latin America 100 million cubic metres of industrial wood and 280 million cubic metres of fuel wood, and Asia 100 million cubic metres of industrial wood and a staggering 560 million cubic metres of fuel wood.

Much of this comes from the rainforests, which are to be found in a belt around the equator stretching from 10 degrees north to 10 degrees south. Although they cover only 8 per cent of the earth's surface, nearly half the wood in the world and at least two fifths of all species of plants and animals live within them.

return, the area in question has to be set up as a national park, and money has to be found to run it properly—something that costs far less than the repayment of the instalments on the original debt. This system is working so well that schemes have already been set up in Bolivia, Costa Rica and Ecuador, and by the time this book is published, there should be another in Peru.

The whole idea of national parks is also being looked at carefully to see how they can be made into a viable commercial proposition. In Panama the Kuna Indians have turned part of their traditional homelands into a national park. They protect it from vandalism and they are free to earn money for it. This idea is so sensible that one cannot help but wonder why other countries are not falling over themselves to do the same thing. In Brazil the government has over-reacted and banned anyone who is not an Indian from entering the traditional lands of the Yanomami.

Conservation organisations are doing superb work in helping national parks. In Peru, Manu national park, thought to be the most diverse area of rainforest in the world, is supported by the World Wide Fund for Nature, and this organisation, in conjunction with the British Overseas Development Agency, works to protect Korup, the lovely forest in Cameroon.

The great problem with these ideas is what to do if the country in which the parks occur reneges on the deal. There is not much point suing, since, if they did not pay the original loans which got them into a mess, they are not likely to take a lot of notice of someone suing them. Another difficulty is the actual running and policing of the parks. Since, as we have seen, the idea of a need to conserve plants and animals does not mean much to many countries where rainforests are to be found, the management of such reserves is generally considered a fairly low priority. There might very well be legislation to ensure that all is done, but I always regard with some scepticism conservationists' jubilation when they hear that such laws have been passed. One does not have to spend much time in the Third World to find out that legislation is meaningless without the will to enforce it. Over and over again one can come across national reserves around the world within whose boundaries blatant and illegal exploitation takes place every day, quite often with the connivance of the relevant government department that should be protecting them. Another problem is the boundaries of these places, which turn out to be surprisingly flexible when it is realised that there is a resource of some value inside the original line. As I said, it is no use telling people what they must do unless an option can be given to them which will put more money in their pockets.

This is perfectly possible. Much of the rainforest is being destroyed for timber and to make charcoal for a variety of other industries. It is probably not very practical to try and replant all the original, forests though it would be great if some replanting could be done. But there is no reason at all why, in all the areas that have already been cleared, plantations of rainforest trees with a commercial value should not be established. This is already happening in some places, and could happen everywhere. There is not going to be a return on the timber for a number of years until the trees are large enough, but in the meantime cash crops could be grown between the seedlings, and livestock could even be kept on the same land provided the baby trees were protected. This would have the added advantage of adding natural fertiliser to the soil. When the timber trees are mature they could be harvested and all the unusable bits could still be burnt as fuel. Each year new areas would be planted so that the trees matured in rotation. Where this is already being done it is working fine and there can be no doubt that tropical hardwood in the future will all have to come from sustainable resources, which is to say that felled trees will have to be replaced so that forests do not disappear.

ALTERNATIVE TIMBER

The other obvious answer is to look at alternatives to the timbers that are taken from the jungles of the world. Throughout Malaysia, Indonesia and other parts of the Far East there are enormous plantations of rubber trees. These are tapped regularly for the latex. After fifteen years, the amount of latex that can be obtained is reduced to a trickle, so the trees are cut down and replaced with a new lot. For many years the wood of the rubber tree has been used by the far-sighted Taiwanese for making crates and pallets, and for mincing up into little chips to fill the space between the veneers of so-called knock-down furniture, which is nothing of the sort, but rather furniture that comes flat in a rupturingly heavy cardboard box, and has to be made up into bookcases and television cabinets. Rubber wood is a perfectly good tropical hardwood which could be put to all sorts of other applications, but has the timber trade thought about it? Well, they have thought about it, and they have all the information they could want about it, and rubber wood is available, but because of the inertia within the industry hardly anyone bothers to import it into the western world. Yet experiments have shown that rubber wood can be used for all sorts of things. It is perfect for broom handles and furniture carcases, and it is ideal for door thresholds and even window frames.

I would be the first to agree that it is of no use for many

As little light reaches the forest floor, it is not surprising that little grows at ground level though numbers of herbs are to be found there. Many of them are relatives of the common ginger, and of that popular house plant, the African violet, or the arum lily.

Many ferns live in this environment, and while most jungle floor plants are necessarily tolerant of low light levels, some, like the filmy ferns, can only exist in shady conditions.

Not surprisingly, virtually all the forest floor plants are fairly small, but occasionally one comes across one of the 50-odd species of bamboo, which are really very large grasses, that occur here and there, especially where part of the forest has been disturbed at some time in the recent past.

Some of the fungi found on fallen tree trunks look like most people's idea of fungi, that is to say, mushroom-like. In addition, bracket fungi are common, while on virtually all the fallen leaves, and indeed on some growing ones, fungi of many species

are abundant. Most look like black or greyish patches and are similar to those that afflict garden plants around the world. Parasitic, or partially parasitic, plants are to be found in the rainforest, such as the members of the mistletoe family. These plants damage their host tree by taking nutrients from it, while their roots can penetrate the tissues of the host. If a tree is heavily parasitised this can be observed in the sparsely distributed leaves, though it is unusual for parasites to cause the death of a host.

Fungi take all shapes and colours and are an essential part of the cycle of the rainforest. This attractive little specimen is in Amazonas, Brazil (*Adrian Warren*)

■

other things, but it is just not exploited as it should be, and if it is ignored by the timber industry it will simply be burnt, and timber will be taken from the forests to be used instead. At the moment it is not the cheapest timber available, but as ramin is banned for export, and maranti and all the other timbers that the industry has taken for granted also become unobtainable, the price will turn out to be increasingly attractive. Furthermore, as consumers begin to refuse timber from non-sustainable resources, it will become all the more desirable. The company that takes a deep breath and dives in now and imports a container-load will be on to a winner. Other countries in Europe buy it, but the UK still does not want to know. Companies like G.S. Supplies in Singapore send out containers all over the place and the demand is increasing, but as yet the only use to which it has been put in the UK is the manufacture of bowls and other

> **Figures for 1980 show that we now consume 3 billion cubic metres of wood a year, which is equivalent to a heap large enough to cover a city the size of Birmingham to a depth of about 80 ft (24 m). Over half of this (54 per cent) is hardwood.**

ornamental household products. When it is stained it looks every bit as attractive as any other wood you care to name, and tests and treatment identify it as a most useful timber. There is a disadvantage, it must be admitted, and that is that the maximum length of available pieces is 6 ft (180 cm), while neither of the two other dimensions can be more than 6 in (15 cm). The timber is sold in lengths of 2 ft (60 cm), 4 ft (120 cm) and 6 ft (180 cm), and I am convinced that there is a great future for the product.

There must be a whole range of other alternatives to tropical forests' timbers that have not yet been examined, and eucalyptus is one of them. Eucalyptus are natives of Australia, though nowadays it is common to see plantations of them all over Asia. Although I do not care to see them everywhere, I would far rather see the timber used to the full than more forests cut down.

South American scorpions tend to be small and insignificant; this large black specimen from the Far East looks dangerous but its sting, though painful, is not fatal (*Peter Tryuk/The Tropical Butterfly Garden*)

(OPPOSITE)
Deep in the jungles of Suriname in South America, male cocks of the rock display at a communal site for the benefit of the rather more drab females (*Adrian Warren*)

■

TOURISM

One obvious way of exploiting rainforests is by tourism. Tourism can be very much of a mixed blessing as a resort can end up with drink cans and kiss-me-quick hats all over the place, but it is perfectly possible to organise the business sensitively. Some countries are so keen to import tourists that they go overboard and destroy all that the tourists come for in the first place. Singapore is rather like this; it has pulled down virtually everything more than twenty years old and rebuilt the place, with the result that many tourists coming to Singapore feel cheated. I love the place dearly but I would be the first person to admit that the town has become just like another Manhattan.

Singapore is a great trading nation now, but package tourists will find little to interest them apart from the superb shopping centres and the diverse range of marvellous restaurants.

The government has realised what is happening, however, and is taking steps to reverse the destruction. Luckily there is still a piece of primary rainforest left at the Bukit Timah Reserve. This is especially attractive as it is rich in animal and plant species. If you take one of the main paths through it, you climb ever upward so that while you start at ground level, you end up looking down into the canopy, which is an admirable way to explore a rainforest—you see the best of everything. If you are interested in natural history, Singapore is a great place to visit as there are plenty of terrific sites for watching animals, a lovely zoo and botanical garden, and a really attractive bird garden at Jurong, to the west of the town. Go and see Singapore if you get the chance—there is all sorts to do, but if you want architecture and culture you might be disappointed.

One of the advantages of sensitive tourism to rainforest areas is that many of the people that actually live there can be used to service the industry, replacing their originally bleak outlook with regard to work. More and more travel companies nowadays are going in for what has come to be known as eco-tourism. Holidays are carefully worked out so that no lasting damage is done to the environment, and the companies promoting this sort of package give a percentage of their income to the countries they are helping to sell. If you are interested in learning more about eco-tourism, get hold of a copy of the *Green Consumer Guide* (see Bibliography) and look through the travel pages, which list the relevant companies. One of the nice things about green holidays to the rainforest is that people who have always been hunters can be used as guides for the parties of tourists, since they are the best naturalists in the world.

The extraordinary spider flower, named for its appearance, grows as high as 8000 ft (2500 m) in the Andes. The drops of moisture give an indication of the high humidity (*Tony Morrison/South American Pictures*)

(OPPOSITE)
In this Waorani lodge on the Cononaco river in Ecuador live twenty-two men, women and children. Their lives are bound up with the jungle in which they live, and they seldom move very far from their home (*Adrian Warren*)
■

In 1975, Britain alone imported 76,800 spotted-cat skins from South America, but, by 1985, the quantity had reduced to a mere 34,520 as a result of new legislation and falling demand.

MEDICINES

As we have seen, many of the plants we have taken from rainforests have been invaluable in the developing of medicines. The people of the rainforest have received virtually nothing from this, despite the fact that in the first place it was usually the locals who pointed the scientists in the direction of a certain plant for a specific purpose. At one time the Wellcome Foundation used to buy curare directly from the Peruvian Indians, but after a time the company managed to synthesise the compound and that source of revenue was cut off from them. Any pharmaceutical company will always try and synthesise a chemical if they can because nobody can prevent a competitor from using a plant from the rainforest or anywhere else for that matter, but a synthetic compound can be patented, and thereafter all the profits belong to the patent-holder.

The New York Botanical Garden have managed to negotiate a rather nice deal with two of the major drug manufacturers in the United States. In return for anything useful that emerges as a result of plants supplied by the botanical garden, the companies have agreed to pay a percentage of the takings from the medicines thus developed as a royalty to the Indians who produced the material in the first place, and towards conservation in the countries of origin. Further such deals could certainly be worked out.

It should not be forgotten that about 70 per cent of the people in Third World countries still use traditional medicines when they are unwell, and many of these are developed from local plants. The Chinese have long had an amazing medical system and wherever one finds a Chinese community throughout the world there are sure to be traditional Chinese pharmacists. They also use many animal products, though it would seem that any beneficial effect reported from the use of these is purely psychological.

In a typical area of one or two hectares of rainforest it is common to find 200 species of tree, compared with four or five in a similar area of temperate forest.

Nevertheless there is still a healthy trade in rhino horn, not as people in the West persist in maintaining, as an aphrodisiac, but mainly as a febrifuge, and for help at the time of a difficult birth. Other parts of the rhino are also used including the urine The gall bladders of bears are also said to reduce high temperatures and are efficacious in treatment of disorders of the liver. Ground tiger bones cannot be bettered for cases of backache, so I have been told, and the only thing that will definitely cure a kidney condition is the appendix of an elephant. On top of that the pharmacists use scorpions, the gall bladders of snakes (especially cobras), centipedes and all sorts of beasties.

Many of the animals used are protected today, but if you think this reduces the chance of finding them in shops, think again. When it comes to rhino horn, the rest of the world has tried to persuade Chineses pharmacists that all sorts of other things will do, and one can find horns and antlers from assorted sheep, deer, antelopes and Himalayan goats, but rhino horn is still very expensive and therefore the most likely to do good. I asked a Chinese pharmacist in Bangkok about three years ago how much rhino horn cost, and he told me that he was currently paying about 100,000 baht a kilo, and at the time there were 37 baht to the pound sterling. It does not need a mathematician to calculate the cost of such a treatment even though the material is grated into very fine powder or flakes before a tiny scrap is sold to the patient. One can even buy tablets allegedly made of rhino horn but I am pretty sure that they do not contain any.

The species of plant used by the Chinese for medicinal purposes are legion, and primitive communities around the world have also developed a considerable pharmacopoeia. Unlike animal-based medicines, virtually all those made from botanical

Fuchsias originate from Bolivia and other parts of the same continent, and nowadays fuchsia specialists are using wild stocks to bring new life into ailing strains of cultivated fuchsias (*Marion Morrison/South American Pictures*)

(OPPOSITE)
The Dayaks make music in their longhouse in Borneo. Dayak lifestyles are changing fast as civilisation brings its advantages into their lives (*Robin Hanbury-Tenison/Survival International*)

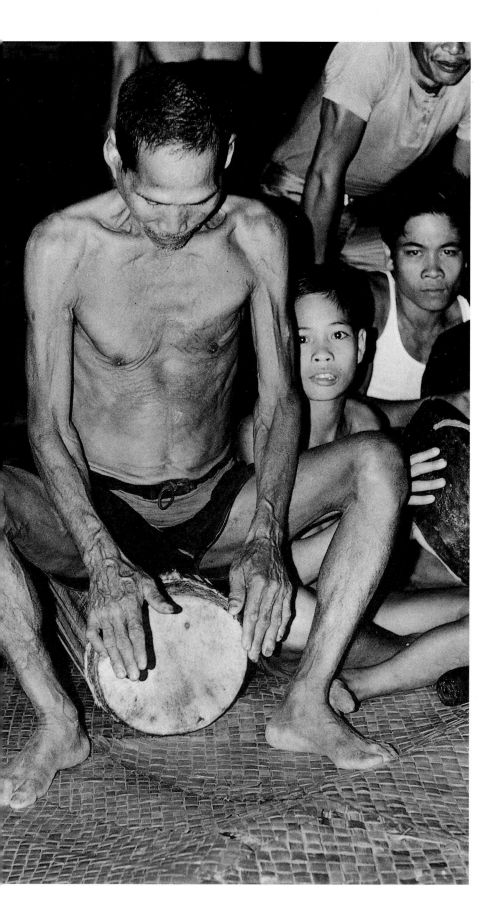

Brazil could rid itself within a month of nearly half its external debt of US$115 billion if it came forward with a verifiable programme for preserving the Amazon. The idea comes from Karl Zeigler, a former American banker who was partly responsible some years ago for arranging at least 30 major loans in Latin America and elsewhere.

His proposals to resolve the Third World debt go far beyond the 'debt for nature' swaps which have been arranged by Unicef, the Dutch government, Conservation International and the Worldwide Fund for Nature. Seldom exceeding US$3 million, these have mostly been imposed on debtor countries including Zambia, Bolivia, Costa Rica, Peru and Ecuador, which have promised to conserve their environments along agreed guidelines laid down by the institutions in return for having their debts written off. But this kind of 'gringo greenmail' was angrily rejected by Brazil's former President, José Sarney.

sources do work and scientific testing shows that the plants used all contain chemicals with a known beneficial effect.

A sensible way, then, of making rainforests cost-effective is surely to develop the ancient herbal medicines of the local people since most of them prefer them and use them anyway. At the moment vast quantities of valuable foreign currency are spent buying modern medicines from Europe and the United States to treat all sorts of conditions in Third World countries. If some of that money was spent developing the culture of medicinal rainforest plants and producing medicines from them that were needed, several advantages would accrue. First, the plants become more valuable because they are being used. Second, they could be made into drugs in rather more controlled conditions to optimise their effect and there would then be no need to import nearly as much medicine from abroad. Third, a country could develop an export trade in these products. There can be little doubt that new drugs would be found that would be of interest to the big multinational manufacturers, and when this happened a royalty system such as that referred to above could be negotiated. Lastly, everyone in the country the plants are found in would become aware of the plants and the need for their conservation and the financial importance of the material, instead of taking them for granted as is done now.

The jungles of the world are packed with attractive plants like this Melastome. Many of our common house plants started life in rainforests, though nowadays they have been bred to withstand central heating and gas fumes (*Brian Rogers/Biofotos*)
∎

There are answers to all the problems facing the rainforests, if only businesspeople would be bothered to think sideways. As it is, virtually all these solutions have been thought up by conservation-conscious scientists.

Of course it would be nice to think that everyone will suddenly see the light and countries around the world will get together and immediately impose a ban on the destruction of all rainforest, but in the meantime all these various options can be implemented immediately.

Certainly the first thing that should be done is for banks and other institutions that are in the business of lending money to refuse to do so any longer to projects that might cause damage to the environment. In addition the Timber Trade Federation should immediately stop the importation of timber that does not come from sustainable resources. Such a ban must come soon anyway, simply because there will no longer be any such timber left. Is it not sensible to stop while we still have stocks that can be used to start commercial plantations?

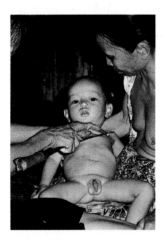

Penan family life in Borneo. It is likely that the life of the little boy will be totally different to that of his parents. Unless logging is stopped now, his forest will be gone by the time he grows up (*Marcus Colchester/Survival International*)

(LEFT)
A long-nosed green tree snake in Borneo. These snakes are very common throughout the Far East. They are mildly venomous, though no threat at all to man, and feed entirely on lizards (*Adrian Warren*)
∎

WHAT IS BEING DONE TO HELP?

A staple food of the Penan tribe of Sarawak is sago, obtained by extracting the starch from the sago palm. This man has just felled a tree in order to obtain the sago. Some forest people in islands further south have always existed principally on sago (*Sahabat Alam/Survival International*)

■

Analysis of a hectare of Peruvian jungle showed that its value was £4,386, while if it was cleared for cattle ranching it would only be worth £1,903.

ALTHOUGH THE SITUATION FACING the rainforests of the world is critical and their destruction continues at frightening speed, it would be wrong to assume that nothing is being done or that the destruction is as fast as it could be. Over the last ten years or so many people have become aware of the imperative need to save what is left of our jungles and to save them now.

Most conservation organisations are doing something towards solving the problem, if only because all the conservation problems in the world interlock with each other constantly. Take for example the Royal Society for the Protection of Birds in Britain. Their main aim is to ensure that birds in the UK are able to get on with their lives without being persecuted and without having their homes destroyed. But many British birds are migrants that regularly make the journey between Britain and the forested countries of west Africa, so the RSPB cannot help but have an interest in the subject. Similarly a body like English Heritage, whose main concern is with historical buildings, is finding that acid rain is causing deterioration of the stones from which many of them are built, the same acid rain that is destroying trees around the world. Some time ago I was working on a season of television programmes about conservation and we were trying to persuade a programme controller that the conservation of cowslips, castles, caracals and corn dollies was all the same thing. He refused to see it, but it is true, and people who belong to any sort of conservation group will often join other apparently unrelated ones.

So while most conservation bodies have some sort of interest in rainforests, some of them are working hard specifically towards halting their destruction. Friends of the Earth has had a rainforest campaign on the go for some little time now, and the

A Wao girl from Ecuador, showing her face paint obtained from local plants (*Adrian Warren*)

■

Tropical forests are vital to the world's climate because they absorb quantities of solar radiation. Once they have gone, far more of the sun's radiation is bounced back from the surface. This is known as the albedo effect, and any increase in it can result in changes in wind currents, disruption in convection patterns, and rainfall in parts of the world seemingly unrelated to the tropics.

The rainforests are also important in balancing carbon dioxide levels. Burning forests releases much of this gas into the atmosphere, and this is helping to increase the 'greenhouse effect'. Drier, hotter climates are already being experienced in many parts of the globe as a direct result.

World Wide Fund for Nature is doing much work on the subject, and has been for years. This international group funds projects in many parts of the world, and is superb at publicising the issues. As mentioned before, some years ago they commissioned a chorale entitled *Yanomamo* about the plight of the Indians of Amazonia. It is sung by a huge choir of schoolchildren, and to listen to it is a powerful and most moving experience. Performances have taken place all over the UK, and in the USA. Wherever the children perform there is a tremendous response. Since then WWF and the same school have done another piece about Africa, and although I prefer *Yanomamo* I also like the African music and some of the drumming makes the hairs on the back of your neck stand up!

A recently set up group, ARK, is also concerned with this area, and the Rainforest Foundation, which is fronted by the singer Sting, is doing much to spread the word as well as working hard behind the scenes. Sting has had the courage to stand up to the Brazilian government in Rio and challenge them to arrest him when he publicised what they were doing to the Amazon forest. I have a lot of time for this organisation, which does not believe in pussyfooting around as so many do, and it seems to me that the time has come when people who care really must stand up and make their voices heard.

The Fauna and Flora Preservation Society has been running a campaign for some years now and they have considerable knowledge and experience in this field.

The International Union for the Conservation of Nature has special expertise in this area and, if you are looking for information for any rainforest project, the IUCN will either be able to tell you what you want to know or will point you in the right direction.

But it is no good everyone knowing what is happening and trying to save monkeys, trees or whatever if the banks and other financial institutions are not made aware of the need to stop funding rainforest destruction projects now. So the Natural Resources Defense Council in Washington is essential, as it lobbies the World Bank and the US government ceaselessly and unmercifully. As I said at the beginning, disappearance of the forests is not just about trees, it is primarily about people, and we should not forget that. After all, it is only natural that of all issues we should be most concerned with those that primarily affect us. It is nice therefore to know that there are organisations working specifically in the field of helping rainforest dwellers. The Foundation of Ethnobiology in England is researching into how the rest of the world can make the most use of the encyclopedic knowledge of the people who actually live in the forests, and they have projects in Ghana at the moment.

A chameleon in Madagascar. The extraordinary chameleons are only found in the Old World. Their tails are prehensile, each eye can be used independently, and they have a limited ability to change colour (*Adrian Warren*)

Survival International is an old, well-established organisation which has been working for years for the rights of tribal peoples of the world. Four per cent of the world's population belong in this category and they are very often treated as obstacles to progress. Survival International has had considerable success, though I am sure they would be the first to agree that they have not had enough. In Venezuela, mining rights which were threatening the life of the local Indians were withdrawn after a campaign of protest. In Brazil the government has agreed to at least do something about the plight of the Yanomami, and in Indonesia after the organisation protested strongly to the United Nations support was given to refugees from harmful government policy in Irian Jaya.

The Forest People's Support Group in London is also concerned with the rights of peoples who live in and around the rainforests, while AMETRA, also in London, aims to revive herbal medicine among the Indians of southern Peru. They are also helping the local people manage the Tambopata Reserve.

It should not be forgotten that zoos around the world are

doing much towards rainforest conservation. In many of them rare and beautiful animals are being bred to save them from extinction, and in some cases, where conditions are right, specimens are being returned to their homeland. And while zoos are conserving animals, botanical gardens the world over are doing the same for plants, and museums are doing what they can to help our knowledge of animals, plants, geology, people and all the other aspects of a rainforest.

All these various groups, zoos and so on are delighted to hear from anyone with serious enquiries and most of them have leaflets, posters and educational material, from books to video tapes. There are schemes that volunteers are always welcome to help with, and if you can do nothing else it is worth joining some of the organisations that you feel suit your interests best, and sending them a donation. Most of them are desperately short of money. Do not forget that the conservation organisations produce catalogues of gifts at Christmas and you can help their work by buying presents for yourself and your friends from these catalogues. You will find addresses for the organisations mentioned above, together with other useful contacts, at the end of this book.

> **Six petroleum nut trees from the Philippines can provide 70 gallons (300 litres) of oil for cooking or lighting, and could thus alleviate the crisis caused by over-collection of fuel wood.**

One of the most vital weapons in the fight against the destruction is education, and by learning as much as possible on the subject everyone will be in a position to talk to friends and tell them why it is important to them that they should care about the disappearing jungles. Another good idea if you are an outgoing sort of person is to contact a local radio station and suggest you do a talk for it, but for goodness sake do your homework first. There is nothing more irritating to a programme producer than to have a guest turn up who has never heard the programme to which he or she is going to contribute and consequently does not know what is expected of him or her. Listen to the programme several times, see how long interviews are, make sure you know your subject, and go along.

Please remember, though, that the producer and presenter of the programme may not be in the least interested in rainforests, and they may know that their audience is far more concerned about the latest pop record or the fact that a celebrity is going to be in the area the following day to open a shopping complex. Therefore there is no point going on air feeling terribly solemn and worthy, caring desperately about your subject and determined to get the sermon across whatever.

An interview will work far better and have more impact on the listeners if you treat it in humorous fashion with plenty of jokes, and put in local-interest points here and there. A really great, tear-jerking anecdote somewhere in the middle helps as well, and do finish with your best gag so that later everyone who

A woman of Sarawak on her way to do some fishing. She carries a fine net and a basket to keep her catch. Although there are some splendid, large fish in the rivers of her homeland, the catch usually consists of tiny fish, which are often opened up and dried in the sun (*Sahabat Alam/Survival International*)

■

listened to the programme remembers what has been said. If you do not approach the programme like this, do not think for a moment that your listeners will stay with you till the end just because what you are talking about is important to you. They will have switched to another channel within a minute. Not only that, but the radio station will not ask you back again. Remember that the station is in the business of entertainment. Whatever else its programmes are about, they must be entertaining.

Bear all this in mind and you will find it easy and will enjoy what you are doing. The final thing to remember is never to stop talking. What may sound a short pause to you can seem to go on for ever and, once you have 'dried' once, you are likely to do it again. Then you start umm-ing and er-ing and the interview ends in a mess. If you really do get stuck at some point, it is perfectly alright to say to the interviewer, 'I'm sorry, I've forgotten what you asked me; tell me again.' It is a good idea at first, until you have developed confidence, to write on a piece of paper two or three points that could be used but do not have to be. Then, if you do forget what you are talking about, simply refer to your bit of paper. If you do not use them no one will know, but they will act as a safety blanket. See if you can find a friend who will record the programme for you and when you get home listen to it. It will make you squirm and you will kick yourself for lost opportunities, but that does not matter. Listen to the way it has gone and you will learn valuable points for the next time. Local radio is often pleased to have input of this nature and it is a shame not to use the medium, but if you are the sort of person who would not feel happy taking part in a programme ask another member of your family or a friend to help you.

Many individuals are amateur naturalists who keep animals or plants in their homes. If you do this, another way you can help if any of your charges are rainforest species is to do all you

As a substitute for petrol, fuel equivalent to one million barrels of crude oil can be obtained from 1200 acres of ipilipil trees.

can to breed them in captivity. There are two great benefits to this. The first is that the more stocks there are of animals and plants that are fast disappearing, the better, and the second, and very important point is that someone maintaining a breeding programme like this has a wealth of valuable information at their fingertips. It is essential to keep notes on everything that happens. You might think that every last fact has already been discovered about the species you are keeping, but you would be astonished at the gaps in our knowledge, and by accident you might stumble on something for which other people have been searching for years. That has happened repeatedly. Join one of the reputable societies that produce a journal through which information is disseminated. Two that immediately come to

mind are the British Tarantula Society and the Marmoset and Tamarin Breeders League, but there are plenty of others.

If you are new to the idea of breeding plants and animals and would like to try, join a society first since many species are now protected and all sorts of licences may be needed to hold stocks, or indeed the species might not be available at all. Another point to bear in mind is cost. Some plants may cost you £5, but whereas twenty years ago you could buy a squirrel monkey for £8, a pair of them today will cost you several hundred pounds and on top of that you will need to build expensive housing for them which will include a centrally heated unit. In addition there are all the usual expenses such as veterinary bills and food.

A Sarawak Indian fishing for his supper. Catches are often meagre, but fish are a useful protein supplement to a diet that can be deficient in meat. Animals are not easy to catch (*Sahabat Alam/Survival International*)

(PREVIOUS PAGE) These Philippino pod katydids may seem brightly coloured on the dark-green leaf. In reality they are superbly camouflaged and only reveal their presence when they move (*Peter Tryuk/The Tropical Butterfly Garden*)
∎

One thing that everyone can do is to make their feelings known to the people who influence things. Write to or telephone the embassies of the countries you are concerned about. You may very well get a brush-off, but if enough people contact them they will begin to get the message, Write also to banks, especially your own bank, and tell them very politely but firmly what you think of banks that are helping to destroy the rainforests, and tell them why you think that. Suggest that you might care to move your money elsewhere. Do the same with any investments to ecologically sound funds.

Next time you are looking to buy something that may come from rainforests, ask about it, and refuse to buy it if it is from a non-sustainable resource. You can always find alternatives.

When it comes to house plants you are fairly safe, as nearly all of them have been bred in captivity, but do make a point of enquiring about air plants and the rarer cacti as these are sometimes taken from the wild. Air plants in particular are susceptible to this sort of exploitation, especially if they are in flower, because it takes them several years between the time the seed germinates and the time the plant finally flowers and it may not be worth the while of the nursery to keep them this long.

Drop a line to your Member of Parliament and tell him or her that you do not think the government is doing enough about the problem, but whenever you contact any of these

This calceolaria is a relative of the common house plant, and is found in the forests of the Andes in South America (*Marion Morrison/South American Pictures*)

(OPPOSITE)
This flatworm, or planarian, lives in the forest of Trinidad. Many wormlike animals have fascinating colours and shapes, and the jungles of Trinidad are packed with equally interesting animals (*Adrian Warren*)

■

For every cubic metre of timber that is removed, a quarter remains after processing in the form of chips, small branches and leaves. This wastage is equal to 100 million cubic metres annually.

people do make sure you know your facts thoroughly. There is nothing likely to weaken a cause so much as those who represent it not knowing what they are talking about. Write to your MP after some story about the government being green hits the headline, and do not be afraid to write to him or her again. It is easy for MPs to ignore a single letter but far more difficult to pretend that a nine-foot-high stack of them is not blocking the door when they want to go home at night.

Watch for stories in the media and then contact whoever put it out. Nothing is more impressive than a television programme or a newspaper being able to say that after the story of the rainforests they received thousands of letters.

Hold fund-raising activities and send the money to your favourite conservation charity.

One good idea is to get hold of a copy of *The Good Wood Guide* from Friends of the Earth, whose address you will find at the back of this book, and read it. It does make pretty boring reading because the layout is dreadful but the information is all there. Write and ask the companies who are listed as still using rainforest timbers if they have done anything to clean up their image since the book appeared, and you can also contact local builders to see whether they are using tropical hardwoods from

The almost mythical Rajah Brooke's birdwing from Borneo must be one of the most spectacular butterflies in the world. Though these insects are now strictly protected, mounted specimens still turn up in souvenir shops around the world (*Adrian Warren*)

(OPPOSITE)
The attractive plumes of the rain tree can now be seen all over the tropics where it is often grown for ornamental purposes. It originated in Central America (*Tony Morrison/South American Pictures*)

non-sustainable resources. You can then tell them about the alternatives.

When you go on holiday abroad next time, if you possibly can, visit somewhere where you can see rainforests. Not many years ago the difference in cost between such holidays and a spell in Torremolinos was vast but today by shopping around you will find that the two can be remarkably similar in price. When you go, do not stay in your hotel complex all day. Make a point of getting out into the jungle. It is not too hot, and after all you did go there for the sun. Take plenty of photographs, which will be far more interesting when you get home. A picture of you patting an elephant or standing beside an enormous tree covered in ferns will have far more impact than yet another photograph of you on the beach. I guarantee that you will enjoy your time far more than you could on the Mediterranean. Send me a postcard!

When you do look at holidays next time, try going through *The Green Consumer Guide* (see Bibliography) and booking through one of those companies that specialise in eco-tourism and give a percentage of their profits towards conservation of the

places to which they take their customers.

Next time you go to a zoo, look especially at the rainforest animals. Remember that this might be the only chance they have of surviving at all. I have no time for the current feeling among people who should know better that all zoos are doing more for conservation and education than you might imagine. Some collections are richer in jungle species than others. Kilverstone Wildlife Park in Norfolk only stocks Latin American species, and the Jersey Wildlife Preservation Trust in the Channel Islands does great work on saving endangered species from rainforests and other areas. They also run courses at which zoo staff from many Third World countries can find out how to do things properly. At the Jersey Zoo they have a great group of gorillas, and orang-utans, while they breed Bali mynahs which in their Indonesian home are having a hard time, and Mauritius pink pigeons which are now being returned from Jersey to restock the island whence they originated.

Good zoos take an interest in plants as well, but do not forget to visit botanical gardens. There is nothing more pleasing than entering the tropical house in Kew Gardens on a February

The spectacular Angel Falls in Venezuela were discovered in 1930 by a pilot, Jimmy Angel. They are the world's highest waterfall. The water drops 3212 ft from the plateau of Auyantepui (*Adrian Warren*)
∎

The Nation, one of Thailand's major newspapers, reported in September 1988 that the skins of 200,000 endangered South American crocodiles had been tanned in Thailand and exported to Japan in an operation involving Thai forestry officials.

The Nation also reported that, although Thailand has signed the Convention on International Trade in Endangered Species (CITES), local law provides no protection for animals from other countries, despite the fact that this is precisely what CITES is about. It was estimated that the skins had resulted in an order of at least 100 million baht (US$ 4 million).

morning when there is snow on the ground. Instantly you are taken to the other side of the world, deep in the jungle. There even used to be a robin that lived in the old greenhouses—he may have moved when the new range was built, but he used to add a lovely bit of movement and song to what is otherwise a silent environment. Kew is a great place, and what is more you only have to pay a few pennies to enter; it must be the cheapest day out anywhere. It is enjoyable and it is educational, and the more you can learn about forests the more confidently you can tell others about them.

The strange thing about the jungles of Kew Gardens is the assortment of plants from rainforests all over the world. When you are used to the jungles, say, of south-east Asia it is a funny feeling to see all sorts of plants together. There is really no pleasure to match spending time in a rainforest. It is even a wonderful feeling to wake up early in the morning deep in the jungle, roll out of your hammock and sit nursing the first cup of tea of the day. Well, to be perfectly honest the first few minutes are not that much fun since it can get jolly cold at night. But once the first chill has worn off, the early morning without a doubt is the best time when all the diurnal animals are waking up as well. Mind you, nights have their moments as well and though I feel I am pretty familiar with any animals I am likely to come across, there have been times when I have woken at night to an eerie howl and the hair on my scalp has stood up. It always turns out to be something harmless.

Contrary to what some writers of a generation ago would have you believe, you are not going to be torn to pieces by a tiger in the jungle. I have woken up once to see a jaguar lying on the ground not many yards away, completely unconcerned about my presence, though I am sure that had I moved he would have been gone in an instant. To lie quietly and watch something like that is an experience like no other.

There is never any need to carry a firearm, though the people who advise you to do so are those from the towns in the countries where jungles are found, which just shows how little they know about the animals on their doorstep. The only times I have been afraid have been those occasions when I have been swimming in tropical seas. I am not a good swimmer anyway and do not feel confident in water, and to swim along through murky water and not be able to see what is beneath you is frightening, though I think the worst experience is to swim along a coral reef and then look over the top of a hedge of coral to find there is an enormous drop on the other side, into cold, black, bottomless darkness. That is something that gives me the horrors. I would rather have a nice friendly jungle any day.

Some of my favourite jungles are in Thailand. But like

Plants in a rainforest are not just a meaningless, higgledy-piggledy collection. Each has evolved in a special way to survive in different parts of the forest. To make sense of the luxuriant growth, it is a good idea to examine the different types of plant to be found.

The most obvious are the trees. In one or two hectares it is common to find 200 species of tree, compared with four or five species in a temperate forest. However, trees of a single species are not usually found clumped together in groups; they generally occur singly, and this is thought to be so that insect predators with highly specific preferences for feeding on a single species are not so easily able to damage the population of trees in an immediate area. Rainforest trees do not generally produce new leaves continuously throughout the year. Instead, the young leaves grow in flushes once, or maybe twice a year, sometimes only on part of the tree. Trees can grow to a

An exquisite pattern of pepperomia leaves spread along the trunk of a tree (*Heather Angel*)
■

height of 197 ft (60 m) and have a diameter of 5 ft (1.5 m) and most of them are evergreen though they shed leaves continuously.

After the trees, perhaps the climbers appear to be the most obvious plants from the floor of the rainforest. They start as a rosette of leaves on the ground and they may remain so until a tree nearby falls and lets in light, at which stage they suddenly shoot upwards at such a speed that it is almost possible to watch some of them grow. At this stage they have no branches and their leaves are usually few and far between.

As soon as one of these climbers finds part of a taller tree it uses it as a support to reach further towards the sun. Means of support vary. Sometimes the plant will wrap itself round the trunk and branches of the host, or it may have tiny hooks or suckers which enable it to hold on. When it reaches an area of more light the nature of the plant changes, and it might branch, grow more or different leaves, and perhaps start to produce flowers. These climbers are often referred to as lianas and they do no harm to their hosts as such, though if they are very large and grow up a small tree, they may pull it down simply because of their weight. Some of these climbers are covered in savage thorns.

A further type of rain-forest plant appears at first sight to be a climber. These species are known as strangling figs and are completely different. Though they might not seem to be, they are actually trees which grow when a seed germinates in someplace like the fork of a bigger tree.

To begin with, they are epiphytic shrubs, and as they grow they put down aerial roots. Often these form a network around the host tree, grafting together wherever they touch each other, until a basket-like frame-work surrounds the host. At one time it was thought that these plants caused the death of the host by strangling it, but we now know that this is not the case. The aerial roots can become quite substantial in time and appear to be the trunks of the plant. Several species of these strangling figs are commonly sold as house plants. Perhaps the commonest is the weeping fig, which has become very popular in recent years as a house plant.

The only monkeys to have prehensile tails are in Central and South America. In the rainforests of this region, monkeys like this woolly monkey are hunted as food by the forest dwellers (*Adrian Warren*)
■

To many people, sloths are the most extraordinary of animals, yet they are superbly designed for the life they lead. There are only two species of sloth, named the two-toed and the three-toed, from the number of digits on the fore limbs. They hang upside down beneath the branches of rain forest trees in Latin America, living on the leaves of the *Cecropia* tree.

Since they spend virtually all their time upside down the hair grows from a central parting along the midline of the ventral surface. It often looks green from a distance because it is inhabited by a species of algae.

everywhere else they are vanishing. Last November 232 people in the south of the country died, hundreds are still missing and a quarter of a million were made homeless when floods caused by the monsoon left vast areas of land under water. The floods were due entirely to the hillsides having been stripped due to illegal logging. The deputy interior minister of Thailand, Trairong Suwannakhiri, said at the time, 'Nature has delivered its message to the entire nation that it can no longer take the rape and plunder...levelled at it.' He asked for international aid, and as always it was forthcoming, but, oh, how much better it would be if we would stop the madness now rather than try and patch up the mess afterwards.

It would be wrong to end on a low note. Much still needs to be done, but the work of caring, knowledgeable conservationists is beginning to make its mark.

Vietnam, poor Vietnam that has really suffered since the early 1960s in one way or another, was defoliated by the Americans during the war. The number of plants and animals that must have been killed does not bear thinking about but, if you do want to think about it, someone once calculated that a single acre of forest contains 6 million spiders. If you add to that the insects, the birds, the snakes, the mammals, the snails, the frogs....You could go on for ever, but if you look at it this way the numbers must be incalculable. Today Vietnam is beginning to pick itself up again. Professor Vo Quy, the author of *The Birds of Vietnam* and other books, is the driving force behind a scheme to replant the country with 500 million trees. It will be a long time before they are a forest, but it is a start.

Another story that is only just being reported as I write is that a meeting of the International Tropical Timber Association, which represents members of the trade both in the importing countries as well as those in the places that supply the timber, expressed their concern about the situation. Professor Duncan Poore, a British authority on tropical timber, has shown that 99.8 per cent of tropical hardwoods currently in use are produced in an ecologically destructive manner. The ITTA decided that it would like to institute a seal of approval for timber produced from sustainable resources in future, and as a start a team of investigators was to go to Malaysia to check on the destruction of the rainforests in Sarawak. The team would perhaps be headed by Lord Cranbrook who is well known and respected for his interest in rainforest conservation. What is more, all this was to happen quickly, which is unusual, as a report had to be made of the team's findings at the next meeting of the ITTA at Yokohama in October 1989.

The ITTA has also been putting money into conservation projects. A sum of $4.7m has been set aside for a study of the

The beautiful little stinkhorn fungus is so called because of the odour of rotting carrion that it exudes. This smell attracts insects to propagate the spores (*Brian Rogers/Biofotos*)

■

possibility of rehabilitating the logged-over forests in Asia and the Pacific, for a study of natural forest management in Malaysia, and for research and pilot activities in damaged areas in East Kalimantan in Indonesia. The ITTA is made up of all sorts of people and when the organisation asked for money to help fund these projects together with another in Brazil for which they have as yet insufficient funds, Switzerland, Holland, Finland and Japan agreed to put money into this work. The EEC sniffed, lifted its nose in the air and said huffily that it would not fund any ITTA conservation or research projects. Mind you, I would have thought that the ITTA could have extracted some more money from the trade itself, for, although $4.7m seems a great deal, the trade is worth billions annually.

It is only pressure from the individual that is going to change such ludicrous thinking. Sometimes the person in the street feels helpless in the face of politicians and big business, but perseverance pays off. The World Bank, public enemy number one in conservation terms, in the face of mounting criticism has increased its team of environmentalists from seven to forty.

Even Brazil, one of the least concerned of all parties about the way our forests are vanishing, has announced a long-awaited set of conservation measures. Seventeen presidential decrees and seven parliamentary bills make up a package which includes a ban on tax incentives for cattle ranching, a couple of national parks in the forest and an environmental preservation fund. Political opponents claim that the measures are inadequate, but of course they would. It is a rare politician who cares more about the country than about the chance of showing the party in power in a bad light. On this occasion they are right and the measures are probably fairly ineffective even if they can be implemented, but at least it is a start and the government has shown that it is beginning to take note of international pressure, because you can be sure that nothing would have happened if there had been none.

The World Wide Fund for Nature spends its time beavering away in different parts of the world, and it has achieved modest success in Niger where it encourages local communities to build their houses of mud bricks instead of from timber as previously. Not only does this save trees but, perhaps more importantly, for the first time the people concerned have begun to think about trees and the need to save them.

In the spring of 1989 the big fashion shows in Milan went green for the first time and promoted a rainforest conservation image, and many leading designers deliberately took the decision not to use fur in their collections. Not everyone felt the need to join in, and MaxMara, Erreuno and Fendi showed designs

One of Mexico's leading ecologists, Gabriel Quadri states that not long ago 54 million acres (21.8 million hectares) of rainforest covered the country. Now there are only 4 million acres (1.6 million hectares).

(RIGHT)
Orchids, ferns and other epiphytes crowd the branches. Some bromeliads will even establish themselves on telegraph wires and can be commonly seen in places like Trinidad (*Brian Rogers/Biofotos*)
■

Many rainforest plants are epiphytes. They grow from seeds which have been deposited in hollows between branches of trees or in grooves and cracks of the bark. An epiphyte does not do any harm to its host plant, it merely uses it as a base. All the necessary nutrients are obtained from the air and rain water, together with any organic matter that might be deposited on the leaves. Many epiphytes are bromeliads, sold today as house plants under the trade term 'air plants'. Most epiphytes grow in the form of a rosette with a vase in the centre which fills with water. In and around this tiny reservoir small frogs and other animals sometimes live their entire lives. Almost all the bromeliads are to be found in the New World, where some species will grow on any suitable support, including telegraph wires.

Many orchids are epiphytes, as are some unlikely plants including succulents and the so-called flamingo flower.

From man's point of view termites are very destructive, but in a forest they are invaluable in breaking down fallen trees. This is a nest of termites in Venezuela (*Adrian Warren*)

(OPPOSITE)
The forests of Costa Rica are rich in flowering plants, like this unidentified member of the lily family (*Brian Rogers/Biofotos*)

■

sporting mink, beaver and fox. The Russian fur firm Sokuzpushnina joined forces with the Italian designers Gianni Versace, Gianfranco Ferre and three others, and in the face of considerable public opinion showed only real furs, but if their customers continue to refuse to buy furs they will have to change their attitudes. One rarely sees a fur coat in public these days simply because it has come to be regarded as a crass, tasteless thing to wear.

The International Union for the Conservation of Nature, the United Nations Environmental Programme and the WWF have come up with three basic principles for the way we exploit our planet. These state that we should not exploit natural stocks of animals and plants so extensively that they are unable to renew themselves and therefore ultimately disappear, we must not so grossly change the face of the earth that we interfere with the basic processes that sustain life, and we must do our utmost to maintain the diversity of the animals and plants that live on the earth. What could be more reasonable than that? Conservationists are often regarded as cranks by the people who feel they are threatening their profits, but true conservationists are eminently reasonable and practical.

Jungles are still disappearing fast but provided we stop the destruction now we can all manage to sustain life as it is and maintain our standards of living. We then need to begin replanting trees, as they are in Vietnam, and in a century we will look back and wonder what the panic was all about. The future of the world lies in the hands of all of us and it will do no good leaving it to somebody else. We have looked at ways in which every single person can be involved, and many of them involve no pain. That is important because not everybody wants to sit buried up to their neck in jungle soil in the face of oncoming contractors' bulldozers as some people have done.

If you want to persuade people that saving our rainforests matters you should remember two basic principles. The first is that it should cost them nothing, and the second is that they should be able to get some kind of profit out of whatever they do. Some people will help even at no profit to themselves, but the chances are that they will do this of their own accord without your influences. It is important to influence those who do not know or do not care.

Tropical rainforests are by far the richest habitat on earth. Over half the world's species of animals and plants live in them.

INDEX

Acid rain, 136, 174
Africa, 23, 36, 40, 49, 59, 63, 65, 67, 92–4, 120, 128, 133, 136–9, 160, 177 *see also individual headings*
Afrormosia, 79
Agland, Phil, 49
Agwantibo, 63
Akha tribe, *121*
Amazonia, *12*, 15, 24–32, 41, 49, 50, 80, 100, 127, 138, 159, 177
America, Central, 23, 59, 65, 66, 74, 80, 96, 110, 120, 133, 138; South, 24–32, 34–5, 51, 53, 59–61, 65–8 *passim*, 70, 80, 96, 101, 105, 110, 120, 133, 138, 160 *see also individual headings*
AMETRA, 178
Amphibians, 52 *see also individual headings*
Angel, David, 188; Falls, *189*
Angsirichivda, Boonlert, 85
Ants, 46, 84, 86–7
ARK, 177
Asia, 32–6, 41, 51, 55, 60, 63, 65, 67, 70, 139, 160, 164, 166 *see also individual headings*
Asmat tribe, *119*
Attenborough, David, 49
Australia, 23, 40, 42, 51, 98–9, 136, 139, 143, 166
Azadehdel, Henry, 52

Bamboo, 164
Bangladesh, 105, 119, 128, 139
Bates, Henry Walter, 32
Bats, 38–40, *38*
Barclays Bank, 154
Beetles, 29, 40, 46, *47*, 69, *71*, 74
Belize, 60, 114, 138
Birds, *19*, 24, 35, 41, 49, 51, 63–8, *65*, 83, 85, 92, 98, 113, *167*, 174 *see also individual headings*
Bjelke-Petersen, Sir Joh, 143
Bolivia, 138, 160, 171
Boni tribe, 53
Brazil, 15, 40, 45, 46, 51, 55, 61, 66, 69, 80, 88, 91, 92, 98, 101, 104, 108, 116, 121–3, 127, 133, 138, 143, 147, 153, 154, 159, 160, 171, 177, 178, 194 *see also* Amazonia
Breeding, captive, 182–3
Bromeliads, 47, 80, 185, 195
Buri, Katy, 42–3, 120; Rachit, 33
Burma, 41, 139
Burning, 133; slash and, *106*
Burton, John, 56
Bushbabies, 63
Butterflies, 8, *8*, 28, 34, 40, *86*, *186*
Byrne, Richard/Jennifer, 63

Cameroon, 49, 133, 138–9, 160
Centipedes, 69
Ceylon/Sri Lanka, 54, 101, 139
Chameleon, Madagascar, 39, *178*
Chimpanzees, 40, 56, 63, 128
Chipko movement, 105
China, 51, 139, 170

CITES, 60, 114–16, 133, 188
Climbers/lianas, 35, 46, 79, 191
Cockatoos, 41, 66
Colchester, Marcus, 151
Colombia, 96, 138
Conservation, 14, 15, 19, 42, 104, 113, 114, 119, 131, 138, 143, 147–9, 157, 160, 171, 174–98; International Union for, 177, 196
Costa Rica, 40, 138, 160, 171
Crocodiles, 71, 143, 188; crocodilians, 52, *53*
Cuba, 40

Dalyell, Tam, 153
Dani tribe, *90*, *91*, *150*
Dayaks, *148*, *171 see also* Penan
Debt, 32, 147, 151, 159–60, 171
Deer, Fea's muntjae, 41
Denis, Armand, 37
Deshmukh, V. M., 36
Dietz, Lou Anne, 61
Disease, human, 42, 88, 98, 104

Ecuador, 48, 138, 160, 171
EEC, 194

Figs, strangling, 80, *82*, 191
Fish, 27, 32, 50, 51, 179
Flatworm, *184*
Flora, *14*, 27, *36–7*, 46, *47*, *73*, 79, *83*, *87*, *117*, 123, 164, *170*, *173*, 185, *185*, *190 see also individual headings*
Forest People's Support Gp, 178
Foundation of Ethnobiology, 177
Friends of the Earth, 144, 174, 185
Frogs, *14*, *21*, *29*, *31*, 39, 40, 47, 52, 74, 77, 96, *96*
Fruit, 30–1, 35, 73–4, *74*, 76, *76*, 79, 80, 81, 110
Fungi, 46, 123, 164–5, *164–5*, *194*

Ghana, 139, 177
Gibbons, 56, 59
Ginger, 79, *116*, 164
Goodall, Jane, 128
Gorillas, 37, 39, 40, 56, *57*, 133, 187
Gray, Robin, 42
Greenhouse effect, 133, 136, 157, 177
Guatemala, 34, 60, 138
Guiana, British, 60, 138; French, 41–2, 53, 68, 104, 138

Hirsiwa-Hasegawa, Mariko, 63
H'mong tribe, *32*
Hoatzin, 30, 65, *65*
Holland, 133, 194
Hummingbirds, 41, 65, 83, 91, 153

India, 23, 35–6, 59, 63, 70, 74, 104–5, 139, 149, 151, 153–4, 156–7
Indians, Amazonian, *13*, 26–7, 32, 41–2, *43*, 48, 51–2, 55, 76, 78, 79, 88–9, 91, 92, 94–6, *95*, 98, 104, 136, 177; Kayapo, 15; Oyampi, 92; Wai Wai, 92; Waorani, *89*, *97*, *104*, *137*, *142*, *168*, *176*; Wayana, 104; Yanomami, 91–2, 160, 178
Indonesia, 23, 31, 36, 40, 41, *44*, 56, 59, 66, 67, 70, 76, 92, 101, 118, 119, *123*, 133, 139, 147, 159, 164, 178, 194
Insects, 7, 16–17, 27, 30, 40, 49, *180–1*

Ivory Coast, 25, 76, 79, 139

Jaguars, 60, 70, 188
Japan, 122, 136, 149, 194
Jersey Wildlife Preservation Trust, 51, 61, 187

Kenya, 32
Kew Gardens, 83, 187–8

Langurs, 59, 85
Lemurs, 40, 62, *62*, *146*, *159*
Lilies, 41, 79, 83, 164, *197*
Lime, Otavio Moreira, 15
Lizards, 28, *28*, 34, 70–1
Logging, 75, *75*, 99, 102, 104–5, 107–8, *113*, *115*, 116, 118, 120, *123*, 136, 151
Lorises, 63
Ludwig, Daniel K., 121

Madagascar, 39, 40, 62, 78, 139
Malaysia, 23, 27, 33, 41, 43, 49, 55, 59, 76, 80, 98–9, 101, 102, *112*, 116, 120, 133, 139, 140, 151, 159, 164, *179*, *183*, 192, 194
Markham, Clement, 101
Mauritius, 40
McLure, Elliott, 49
Medicines, 35, 36, 78–9, 120, 133, 169–73, 178, 187
Mendes, Chico, 104
Mexico, 69, 138, 147, 194
Millipedes, 69
Mining, 110, 121, 147
Mitchell, Andrew, 49
Monkeys, 8, 30, 34–5, 59–61, *58*, *61*, 84, 103–4, 183, *193*
Mynahs, 149–9, 187

Nagagata, Elizabeth Yoshimi, 61
Nepal, 105
Ngam, Harrison, 43
Niger, 194
Nigeria, 76, 139

Ocelot, 68, 70, 100
Okapi, 36–7, 56
Orang-utan, 56, 59, 84, 187
Orchids, *33*, 35, 41, 46, *46*, 52, *120*
Otter, giant, 59

Panama, 127–8, 138, 160
Papua New Guinea, 62, 92, 136, 139
Parks, national, 15, 160, 194
Parrots, 41, 45, 51, 66, 100, 115
Penan tribe, 98, *99*, *99*, 140, *140*, *148*, *173*
Peru, 78, 138, 160, 171, 174, 178
Periwinkle, 78, 120
Philippines, 68, 76, 92, 139
Pigeon, pink, 51, 187
Pigs, 67
Poisons, 96–7
Poore, Duncan, 192
Population, 52–5, *53*, *54*, 88–106, 136, 149, 178 *see also individual headings*
Puerto Rico, 51, 100, 138
Pulpwood, 80, 88, 108, 121–3, 127, 147
Puma, 67
Pygmies, 92–4, *93*, *94*

Quadri, Gabriel, 147, 194
Quetzal, 34, *34*
Quinton, John, 154
Quy, Vo, 192

Ramin, 147, 166
Ranching, 24, 78, 111, 113, 147, 154, 174, 194
Raoni, Chief, 15
Reafforestation, 32, 40, 78, 164
Rhinos, 70, 170
Rodents, 42, 46, 67, 68
Rwanda, *20*, 56, 139, *161*

Salleh, Kuramudin Mat, 27
Savetsila, Siddhi, 127
Scorpions, *166*
Shrews, 35, 40, 60
Sifaka, *64*
Singapore, 166, 169
Sloths, 39, 62–3, 192
Snakes, *22*, 29, 39–40, *50*, 51, 70–1, 71, 74, 119, *172*
Soil, 45–6, 105, 108, *110*, 111, 145
Spiders, *8*, 29, *29*, 40, 49, 74, *169*, 192
Squirrels, 35, 49, 60
Suwannakhiri, Trairong, 192
Suwannskorn, Phairote, 85
Suriname, 138, *167*
Survival International, 178

Takasaki, Hiroyuki, 63
Tamandua, 63
Tanager, Mrs Wilson's, 29
Tapirs, 67
Tasaday tribe, 92
Tate and Lyle, 114
Tenrec, 40
Termites, 45, *196*
Thailand, 23, 32, 33, 41–3, 59, 76, 85, 119–20, 127, 133, 139, 147, 188, 192
Tigers, 36, 70, 188
Toads, *18*, 29
Tourism, 166, 169
Trade, animals, 85, 102–3, 115–16, 120, 128, 147–9, 151, 183; skins, 69, 169, 188, 196; timber, 67, 81, 147–9, 160, 166, 173, 183, 192, 194; Association, 144, 173, International Tropical, 192, 194
Trees, *15*, 21–3, 45–87, 190–1; banana, 30–1, 110; cannonball, 81; cauliflory, *72*, 79; ceiba, *13*; eucalyptus, 79; hardwoodl, 21, 22, 49, 49, 73, 79; ipilipil, *182*; kapok, 79; palm, *13*, 35–6, *35*, 76, *156*; petroleum nut, 179; rain, *187*; rubber, 55, *55*, 101, 104, 144, 164, 166
Tupaia, 60

USA, 69, 115, 128, 170, 177

Venezuela, *25*, 65, 91, 92, *124–5*, 138, 178
Vietnam, 39, 139, 192, 196

Wellcome Foundation, 169
Wickham, Henry Alexander, 101
World Bank, 141, 177, 194
World Forest 90, 13, 14, 19
WWF, 70, 91, 160, 177, 194, 196

Yapok, 40

Zaire, 94, 139
Zeigler, Karl, 171
Zoos, 61, 133, 178–9, 187

NORTH ATLANTIC OCEAN
IRELAND
U.K.
MEXICO
BELIZE
CUBA
JAMAICA
DOMINICAN REPUBLIC
PUERTO RICO
NICARAGUA
VENEZUELA
TRINIDAD
GUATEMALA
HONDURAS
COSTA RICA
PANAMA
GUYANAS
COLOMBIA
ECUADOR
PERU
BRAZIL
BOLIVIA
PARAGUAY
ARGENTINA
C OCEAN
NIGERIA
GUINEA
SIERRA LEONE
LIBERIA
IVORY COAST
GHANA
BENIN
CAMEROON
EQUATORIAL GUINEA
GABON
ANGOLA
ATLANTIC OCEAN

16 5105